D0548097

Items should

The Book of Lismore

AN INTRODUCTION

By Donald Brady

Waterford County Council 2010

Published by

Waterford County Council
Co. Library, Lismore,
Co. Waterford

© 2010, Donald Brady

ISBN 9780953202270

Produced by Probe Marketing
info@probe.ie

Contents

Dedication

"For my uncle, Francis Joseph Boland and my aunts, Rosaleen and Josephine Boland who are only known to me through my mother's vivid and enthralling memories."

Donald Brady

Acknowledgements

This work has had a long and difficult gestation. My first examination of the Book of Lismore was directly suggested by Mary Houlihan and the Immrama Committee. The work of Macalister, Stokes, Ó Cuív and other major Celtic Scholars provided essential source material.

Evelyn Coady was indefatigable and unrelenting in finding the most archaic but essential references and without her the production of this book would have been impossible.

Lord William Burlington and the staff at Chatsworth House were most helpful and supportive. Father Uinsean Ó Maidín of Mount Melleray Abbey and Paddy Vaughan of the Institute for Advanced Studies were extremely enthusiastic and helpful.

The Mayors of County Waterford, the County Manager, and Director of Services, Denis McCarthy, were at all times committed to this as indeed other heritage projects for the County.

Finally, the production of this work would not have been possible without the support of the entire staff of Waterford County Library Service, particularly Eddie Byrne and my secretary Anne Walsh.

Foreword

Once again, we have to be grateful to Waterford's indefatigable County Librarian, Donald Brady, for yet another publication that celebrates the cultural heritage of Lismore. Following on his Directory of County Waterford writers and the republication of Smith's Waterford, our County Librarian now provides us with a precise guide to the sleeping giant of Carthage's town, the Leabhar MacCárthaigh Riabhach that connects the Franciscan scholarship of Timoleague Abbey, through the Munster MacCarthys, to the living patrimony of the Lismore Devonshires.

The Book of Lismore was twice a gift: firstly, a wedding gift to the son of Diarmait, Lord Carbery, and the daughter of Thomas, Earl of Desmond, and then a son's gift, as a fair bounty of war, from Viscount Kinalmeaky to the Great Earl of Cork at Lismore Castle. When the MacCarthys came banging on the door in 1643, like librarians wanting their book back, not only did Lismore hold fast to its treasure, but Lismore held fast to its new history, its victory of the modern era: the present moment had been ushered in. This is the moment we now live in and this moment, luckily, has preserved the Book of Lismore very well indeed. The one time that the Lismore Devonshires released the book in the Nineteenth Century it was damaged in an embarrassing effort at 'improvement' by a Cork bookseller with more ink than brains – I will let Donald Brady recall that episode in the following pages. Once again, the name of the scholar-antiquarian Eugene O'Curry, that extraordinary man, comes to the fore. O'Curry's work was crucial, both in terms of explication and recovery. The story of the damage to the Book of Lismore is a salutary lesson: it reminds us how important scholarship is; how important academic guidance, learning and Professorial supervision is when handling historical materials. In each generation it is vital that Ireland educates a band of scholars as well as a cadre of art dealers. The urgency of this need for Celtic and linguistic scholars should be urged upon those who fund our University education. As a people we have a wonderful capacity to preserve the emotions of our national history, but we must also preserve the science of that history. We owe this as much to the memory of Eugene O'Curry as to the memory of the MacCarthys of Kilbrittain Castle.

The Book of Lismore is an anthology, an almanac and a cultural primer. Collated and inscribed for a newly married couple of noble blood; a couple who might be expected to lead their people when the time came, a couple who would breed leaders of men in battle and trade, the book is a life-guide. Produced in homage by holy men, it is an Irish lifestyle almanac.

It teaches us the lives of the saints, the glories of Charlemagne, the story of the Lombards, the nine ranks of the celestial hierarchy, Marco Polo's travels, the privileges and stipends of Irish kings, and many other aspects of memory, duty and poetry expected of a noble Irish mind. It aspires to nobility and it was meant to inspire and mature the reader with the grandeur of grand facts and the music of fantastical possibilities.

What Donald Brady has done for us in this new Introduction to the Book of Lismore is to instruct and awaken us, once more, to the genius of the local past. And it is all local, whether in Timoleague Abbey or Lismore Castle: for the territories of the Eoganacht and the Desmonds, like the more recent territories of the Great Earl of Cork, stretched from County Kerry to the mouth of the Suir. Lismore was always one of the great centres of gravity of those historical territories, a locus of learning, worldly power and ecclesiastical authority. Lismore still has the feel of authority about it: the stones, trees, rivers and gardens still make it a capital place.

Its centrality is still preserved, also, in its Library Headquarters for County Waterford. Knowledge radiates still from an old monastic place and the librarians at work there have preserved a timeless heritage of knowledge that belongs, by right, to Lismore. Donald Brady, our County Librarian, has to be thanked once again for reminding us of the wealth of our heritage. He is a worthy follower of the scribes of Timoleague, and the even more ancient scholars of Lismore.

Thomas McCarthy
1st September 2009

Preface

This book has evolved and developed from a paper presented at the Immrama International Festival of Travel Writing some years ago. A request from the event organisers that I deal with the Book of Lismore was readily accepted as, despite over 25 years as County Librarian for Waterford County Council, I knew virtually nothing of the history or indeed the contents of this, one of the most important Irish manuscript volumes.

The challenge, when undertaken, was to grapple with a resource whose contents were largely alien to my knowledge base. I felt like a modern day explorer gone in search of oneself who found that a fuller understanding would require neither a geographical journey nor the undertaking of a course in Eastern mysticism but rather discovered that within our own history and civilization lay an extraordinary rich, deep and valuable resource that could provide an insight into not only from where we have come but more crucially who we are and why we are so.

In recording and highlighting the man made heritage of Ancient and Medieval Ireland little recognition value is required on the mention of Newgrange, the Rock of Cashel or Christ Church Cathedral. Even more recent edifices such as Lismore Castle have now acquired iconic status; this despite the fact that it is known better for its location and site and the history of its occupants rather than any innate architectural merits.

Of our major literary heritage only the Book of Kells, which is primarily noted for its calligraphy and exquisite art work, would feature in such a list. The other major manuscripts of Ireland are largely unknown outside academic circles. These are seldom recorded, bestowed or allowed adequate status in recognition of their level of sophistication unlike the builders of Newgrange over 5000 years ago or those who crafted the Book of Kells. Rather those who produced the Book of Lismore are sometimes considered as slavish replicators of now redundant copy.

---

[1] Yeats, W.B. *Under Ben Bulben* [in] *The Poems Ireland*: Gill and Macmillan, 1983 xxv, 747 p pg. 325.

The Book of Lismore should be considered and studied as the product of a monastic network that covered Western Europe and one of its products, the manuscript, derived from and is the fruit of this Pan-European knowledge resource.

The transfer and transportation of these manuscripts is stunning in a period when networking even across local areas, let alone seas, was assumed to have been tortuous and sometimes non existent. A central facet of these transfers was an evaluation of the merits of particular manuscript tracts. Only those rated of significant value were selected for *"copying"*. Secondly, the pieces of merit frequently attributed as *"copies of originals"* were just as readily altered by the scribes either through personal choice or at the behest of their monastic superiors. Equally, the transfer from oral to written versions frequently necessitated significant stylistic alterations. Finally the transfer across cultural divides inevitably led to conscious or sometimes unconscious transmutation as themes or narrative pieces required conversion to forms which had a familiarity or recognition factor for the new audience and parallels or likenesses were often selected.

Even a cursory examination of the Book of Lismore reveals a unity of design and concept which despite difficulty in understanding the underlying logic for the inclusion of some passages initially, on further study I believe all conform to a unity of purpose – education and illumination.

The survival of the work through the vagaries of time and particularly through the cataclysmic destruction of the Cromwellian period is in itself a critical historical lesson.

That Lewis Boyle, Lord Kinalmeaky, a leader of the new English, who proved ruthless and sometimes inhuman should value and record the preservation of a work in Irish, which he probably understood little of, and despatch it specially to his father, the destroyer of Lough Derg, reflects an acknowledgement of the value of civilization and its products which one might say has been often lacking in our own day (note the destruction of books in Nazi Germany and by the Soviet Authorities).

The literary revival of the late 19th and early 20th centuries led to an advanced exploration of this work. But sadly little study has been done to restore and enhance its undoubted significance in recent years.

While some poems still need to be explored, I hope that this new beginning will lead to further study – it is a start and by no means the final word. The Gaelic literary and linguistic qualities of the work remain for a more practiced eye than mine to pursue and investigate. I feel certain that such an examination will further enhance the status of this incredible book.

Donald Brady

Background

Significant renovations were carried out to Lismore Castle under instructions from the 6th or Bachelor Duke of Devonshire. During these works, in 1814, a walled up section was opened up and within it a box was discovered containing a bishop's crozier and a manuscript codex. The Crozier, now known by its place of discovery, is inscribed to Níall mac meic Aeducáin who was Bishop of Lismore from 1090-1113. The codex was not bound and had been seriously damaged by dampness and rodents.

In his introduction to the replica edition R.A.S. Macalister tells us that the book had been produced as a wedding gift for *"Finghin Mac Carthaigh Riabhach, son of Diarmait an Dúna, Lord Carbery (whose death in 1505 is recorded in the book of Annals); and his wife Caitlín, daughter of Thomas Fitzgerald, 11th Earl of Desmond [1454-1534], who died in the following year."* [2] However, in his exhaustive, technical but eminently plausible and essential study, Brian Ó Cuív casts considerable doubt on this provenance as with many other underlying conclusions set out by Macalister. Ó Cuív suggests that the dedication may not be just to Finghin and his wife but perhaps could also be applicable to Finghin's father and mother as well and states:

> *"It is by no means certain then, that the identification of the lánamha as Finghin Mac Carthaigh and his wife is correct."* [3]

The Mac Carthaigh Clan had been for some considerable time associated with, and patrons of, the Franciscan Monastery of Timoleague and in fact chose its grounds as the family burial place. According to Macalister as the wedding of Finghin took place in 1480 it can be assumed that the book was completed by then. He continues; *"it is commonly and reasonably presumed, but nowhere, so far as I can find, categorically stated, that the book was prepared in the Friary named as an offering to its patron."* [4] Ó Cuív has serious reservations on this analysis stating that the *"only evidence connecting it with that Friary are colophons in Brussels MS 2324-40 where Mícheál Ó Clérigh says that he copied certain items."* [5]

---

[2] *The Book of Lismore. Introduction by R.A.S. Macalister Manuscripts Commission 1950 pg. xii.*

[3] *Observations on the Book of Lismore. Brian Ó Cuív Proceedings of the Royal Irish Academy Section C – Archaeology, Celtic Studies, History, Linguistics, Literature. Vol. 83 C, Number 1. Dublin: Royal Irish Academy, 1983. pgs. 269-292. pg. 270.*

[4] *The Book of Lismore. Introduction by R.A.S. Macalister Manuscripts Commission 1950 pg. xii.*

[5] *Observations on the Book of Lismore. Brian Ó Cuív Proceedings of the Royal Irish Academy Section C – Archaeology, Celtic Studies, History, Linguistics, Literature. Vol. 83 C, Number 1. Dublin: Royal Irish Academy, 1983. pgs. 269-292. pg. 271.*

There are, however, dedications to Finghin and his bride in four of the *"Lives of the Saints"* contained in the manuscript. It is worth noting that in his edition of the *"Lives of Saints"* Stokes states that the text was *"compiled from the Book of Monsterboice and other manuscripts"* [6] but does not provide corroborative evidence for this claim.

The next mention of the Book is, as already stated, made by Mícheál Ó Cléirigh who on 20th of June 1629 copied from it the Life of St. Finnchua. In a letter dated 25th June 1642 from Lewis Boyle Viscount Kinalmeaky to his father, Richard Boyle the Great Earl of Cork, he recounts the capture of Kilbrittain Castle seat of Mac Carthaigh Riabhach and records sending the manuscript to his father at Lismore. When Lismore was attacked in July 1643 it has been suggested that the Book was walled up for safekeeping. However an inscription on the codex suggests that this may not have happened until after 1745. Referring to this *"hibernation"* Ó Cuív first suggests that *"it may be that the Book of Mac Carthaigh Riabhach had a section, now lost, which was added in the sixteenth century"* [7] thus negating this colourful tale of a prolonged incarceration. During the 18th century we are told that the work of Domhnall Ó Teimhinn writing in 1713 indicates particularly in an account of the Story of the Antichrist that he may have had access to the Book of Lismore. Finally in an analysis of the missing pages and their content Ó Cuív suggests that *"some eighteenth-century manuscripts"* may have either directly or indirectly derived from the Book of Lismore.

Following the discovery in 1814, the book was initially kept at Lismore Castle. It is possible that some of the pages were removed during this time. It was later borrowed by Donnchadh Ó Floinn of Cork, and it was he who bestowed the name of Book of Lismore on the codex. He had possession of it from July 1815 to August 1816 and during this period significant damage was done to the book and some of the pages were stolen. On returning it Ó Floinn had had the book bound doing further damage and making its original structure impossible to discern.

In 1839 the RIA borrowed the book to make a transcription and this work was assigned to Eugene O'Curry. He discovered the theft of the folios and made huge efforts over many years to retrieve the missing pages. [8] He claimed that of the 242 folio pages some 42 were missing from the beginning and some others throughout the manuscript. He discovered some missing pages following the acquisition of Sir William Betham's mss collection by the RIA in 1853 and these and others were returned to the document.

---

[6] *Stokes, Whitley. Lives of Saints from the Book of Lismore Oxford: Clarendon Press, 1890 pg. V It would appear that this claim by Stokes is based on the ascription by Brother Ó Buagacháin in the Lives of Saints to have used the Book of Monsterboice.*

[7] *Observations on the Book of Lismore. Brian Ó Cuív Proceedings of the Royal Irish Academy Section C – Archaeology, Celtic Studies, History, Linguistics, Literature. Vol. 83 C, Number 1. Dublin: Royal Irish Academy, 1983. pgs. 269-292. pg. 290.*

[8] *See "Lectures on the manuscript materials of ancient Irish history" Eugene O'Curry Ireland: Duffy (James), 1861 xxviii,722p.*

O'Curry was not aware of, or chose to ignore, the fact that an earlier complete copy of the Book had been made *"It is a beautiful work of calligraphy and a most accurate copy of the whole manuscript, with none of the lacunae unavoidable when O'Curry made his transcript."* [9] Some further restoration of the Book was achieved as Curry comments in an index to his Lectures *"The Cork part of it has been restored to the original Book of Lismore since delivery of these Lectures."* [10]

Subsequently, it is known that by 1930 the book had been transferred from Lismore Castle to Chatsworth, where it has since remained. In the late 1940's the manuscripts was lent to the Irish Manuscripts Commission who, through the British Museum, produced a *"photographic collotype edition in 1950."*

Michael Slavin in his book draws parallels with the Book of Fermoy as *"it was also created for a family"* namely the Roche dynasty, though that manuscript is a later creation completed in the 16th century and is now held by the RIA.

Description

The book is of vellum numbered to page 242. It stands 14 inches high and is 10 inches across *"There are about 40 lines of writing on each page."* [11] As already stated, the original construction of book is *"now difficult to determine."* The numbering was probably originally Roman and Arabic but may have then been converted to Arabic numbering exclusively. In his analysis of the pagination Ó Cuív points out *"furthermore, the total number of folios missing from O'Curry's transcript is in fact sixty-six"* [12] rather than fifty-five. He also states that:

> *"at four points in the manuscript where there are obvious lacuna through loss of one leaf or more, the Arabic foliation continues without interruption".* [13]

Finally he states that rather than 242 *"the last surviving leaf should have been numbered not less than 248".* [14]

---

[9] *The Book of Lismore. Introduction by R.A.S. Macalister Manuscripts Commission 1950 pg. xi.*

[10] *See "The ancient books of Ireland Michael Slavin. Ireland: Wolfhound Press, 2005 x, 198p pg. 80.*

[11] *The Book of Lismore. Introduction by R.A.S. Macalister Manuscripts Commission 1950 pg. xiii.*

[12] *Observations on the Book of Lismore. Brian Ó Cuív Proceedings of the Royal Irish Academy Section C – Archaeology, Celtic Studies, History, Linguistics, Literature. Vol. 83 C, Number 1. Dublin: Royal Irish Academy, 1983. pgs. 269-292. pg. 271.*

[13] *Observations on the Book of Lismore. Brian Ó Cuív Proceedings of the Royal Irish Academy Section C – Archaeology, Celtic Studies, History, Linguistics, Literature. Vol. 83 C, Number 1. Dublin: Royal Irish Academy, 1983. pgs. 269-292. pg. 273.*

[14] *Observations on the Book of Lismore. Brian Ó Cuív Proceedings of the Royal Irish Academy Section C – Archaeology, Celtic Studies, History, Linguistics, Literature. Vol. 83 C, Number 1. Dublin: Royal Irish Academy, 1983. pgs. 269-292. pg. 274.*

In an interesting comment Ó Cuív states:

> *"It has been suggested to me...that there is evidence of the binding of the Book of Lismore three times before the eighteenth century"*, [15]

and he suggests that this may partially explain foliation variations caused by additions and abstractions over time and in one area specifically we are told that study may *"imply prefixing of additional folios on two occasions, fifteen on the first, and seven on the second"*. [16]

According to Macalister the writing was provided by at least three scribes but *"Of the scribes who collaborated in the preparation of the Codex one had the lion's share of the work."* [17] Stokes has stated that the scribes *"were more of less careless and ignorant."* [18] While much of the work has been ascribed to *"Brother Ó Buagacháin,"* Macalister discounts this and states that the scribe *"has merely preserved Ó Buaghacháin's name by copying the signature appended by Ó Buagacháin to his transcript from the wandering MS, which thanks to its theft, had escaped the Monasterboice fire in 1097."* [19] A subsidiary scribe Aongus Ó Callananáin is identifiable as contributing some of the material in the latter sections of the book.

The production of the Book of Lismore should be considered in the context of the development of printing in Europe. Johannes Gutenberg produced his famous bible using movable type in 1455.

[15] *Observations on the Book of Lismore. Brian Ó Cuív Proceedings of the Royal Irish Academy Section C – Archaeology, Celtic Studies, History, Linguistics, Literature. Vol. 83 C, Number 1. Dublin: Royal Irish Academy, 1983. pgs. 269-292. pg. 291.*

[16] *Observations on the Book of Lismore. Brian Ó Cuív Proceedings of the Royal Irish Academy Section C – Archaeology, Celtic Studies, History, Linguistics, Literature. Vol. 83 C, Number 1. Dublin: Royal Irish Academy, 1983. pgs. 269-292. pg. 291.*

[17] *The Book of Lismore. Introduction by R.A.S. Macalister Manuscripts Commission 1950 pg. xiv.*

[18] *Stokes, Whitley. Lives of Saints from the Book of Lismore Oxford: Clarendon Press, 1890 pg. vi.*

[19] *The Book of Lismore. Introduction by R.A.S. Macalister Manuscripts Commission 1950 pg. xv.*

Contents

The book was produced *"comprising some sixteen small independent sections."* [20]   Macalister summarises: *"This would accord with its character, as a compendium of the works of literature, theological, historical or romantic, which the scribes employed or their superiors considered to be most edifying or acceptable for the prince for whose benefit they laboured".* Ó Cuív disagrees with this structural analysis and has suggested that there are some sections which *"clearly overlap"* suggesting that it may have been generated using *"quaternions."* [21]   This analysis was, however, also suggested by Macalister in his comments on the vellum gatherings where he is quite specific on this conclusion.

 According to Macalister the Book *"is unique among Irish codices in that it was prepared, not for the library of a monastery or of a professional but for the use of an intelligent and cultures layman."* [22] Ó Cuív also disagrees with this analysis referencing the Book of Fermoy. Macalister is most likely correct in suggesting that the vellum gatherings to some degree dictated the extent of the text and in some cases the content of particular sequences with abridgements and additional material used to facilitate the process.

> *"The ultimate form of the book thus became a bundle of gatherings, each comprising a complete text, which could be withdrawn individually for study, thus virtually forming a library of just such volumes as are enumerated above; and which, unlike a heavy bound codex, could be handled separately with ease."* [23]

While this analysis of how the Book was intended to be used sounds plausible the arguments of Ó Cuív cast considerable doubt on the analysis.

---

[20] *The Book of Lismore. Introduction by R.A.S. Macalister Manuscripts Commission 1950 pg. xvi.*

[21] *Observations on the Book of Lismore. Brian Ó Cuív Proceedings of the Royal Irish Academy Section C – Archaeology, Celtic Studies, History, Linguistics, Literature. Vol. 83 C, Number 1. Dublin: Royal Irish Academy, 1983. pgs. 269-292. pg. 283.*

[22] *The Book of Lismore. Introduction by R.A.S. Macalister Manuscripts Commission 1950 pg. xvi.*

[23] *The Book of Lismore. Introduction by R.A.S. Macalister Manuscripts Commission 1950 pg. xvi. Enumeration refers to the sections which are detailed through this essay.*

Most of this section has been lost but from the small section preserved it is likely that the original segment equates to the History of the Children of Israel which in the Leabhar Breac fills 22 folios [44] pages. The actual extant Book of Lismore begins with *"This is Patrick's Life; and let every one who shall read give a blessing for the souls of the couple for whom this book hath been written."*

Homily on Antediluvian History

This piece from the Book of Lismore is now unfortunately lost. However, different versions exist in several of the early Irish Manuscript codices including Lebor Gabála Érenn and An Leabhar Breac. The latter version is, according to Macalister, probably very similar to that which was in the Book of Lismore. The loss of this piece is particularly unfortunate as its role in the opening sequence of the various manuscript codices serves in formulating the essential nature of the works.

Its position and prominence is critical in presenting a world view, providing a precise explanation for the history of the people and establishing a raison-d'ê-tre for the creation of the book. While much of the explanation is based on biblical contexts the presentation of this world view should not be considered simplistic. It is worth pointing out that the elaboration of the theory of evolution and particularly the mechanism of natural selection propounded by Darwin was only proposed in the 19th Century. Perhaps a more cogent example concerns the development of the *"Big Bang Theory"* [24] which was only first proposed in 1931 and its appellation dates from 1949.

---

[24] *This cosmological model was first proposed by Father George Lemaître in 1931, though he described it as a "hypothesis of the primeval atom." He suggested that the "evident expansion in forward time required that the Universe contracted backwards in time, and would continue to do so until it could contract no further bringing all the mass of the Universe into a single point, a 'primeval atom.'" It was Fred Hoyle who bestowed on this theory the description "big bang idea" in a BBC radio interview in 1949.*

The tract provides an extremely valuable insight into the evolution of Irish Monastic historiography. It illustrates a depth and sophistication of thought largely unacknowledged to date. This model involves not only the development of three parallel streams of the *"recording"* of history: Annals; Legends and Chronicles [25] [an exploration of these streams is presented in extremely convincing fashion by John N. Radner], but we can also discern a cross-fertilisation or synergetic development of presentation which is perhaps best displayed in parallels with the work of Nennius. [26]

This evolution is further analysed by David Comyn and has direct applicability to this tract and other segments of the Book of Lismore:

> *"Indeed the gradual modification of the language, and the development of good prose narrative form, to which in early times not much attention was given, may be traced from the 'Irish Nennius,' in the twelfth century, through the 'Passions and Homilies' of the Leabhar Breac, some of the 'Lives' of the Book of Lismore and the Loch Cé Annals, to the translators of the Bible, to Carsuel, and to Keating when the evolution was complete."* [27]

A further central feature is the power and depth of symbolic presentation which is essential for a true understanding of the tract and even Macalister in his sometimes literal rendering of text has levelled criticism on the quality of text as in his introduction to Lebor Gabála Érenn:

> *"an artificial composition, professing to narrate the origin of the Gaedil onward from the Creation of the World (or the Flood), their journeyings, and their settlement in 'their promised land.' Ireland. This production was a slavish copy, we might almost say a parody, of the Biblical story of the Children of Israel. The germ which suggested the idea of the writer was undoubtedly the passage in Orosius"* [28]

which appears to ignore possible less literal explanations but does highlight the fact that Irish writers – as many of their European counterparts – undoubtedly used the Bible and other written texts as templates in their search for acceptable historical formulae. In a review on *"The historicity and historiography of Arthur"* Howard Wiseman makes just this point in reference to the Historia Brittonum:

---

[25] Radner, John N. *Writing History: Early Irish historiography and the significance of form.* Ireland: Celtica 23, 1999 pgs. 312-325.

[26] Nennius was a Welsh monk of the 9th Century. His *"Historia Brittonum"* provides a major contribution to the Arthurian legend. The book *"was a compilation of several sources"* and was *"translated into Irish by Giolla Coemgin in c. 1071 and this version is the earliest extant example of the original. In his attempts at national vindication "Nennius makes several attempts to trace the history of the Britons back to the Romans and Celts through his empirical observations of what he refers to as 'the marvels or the wonders of Britain".*

[27] Comyn, David [in] The History of Ireland by Geoffrey Keating Vol. I U.K.: Irish Texts Society, 1902 pg. viii.

[28] Lebor Gabála Érenn: The Book of the Taking of Ireland Part I edited and translated with notes etc. R.A. Stewart Macalister Dublin Irish Texts Society 1938 Pg. xxxi [Paulus Orosius (c. 375-418 A.D.) was an historian, theologian and follower of Augustine of Hippo. His central work Historiarum Adversum Paganos Libri VII ('Seven Books of history against the Pagans') was written in response to the thesis that the decline of the Roman Empire was a consequence of its adoption of Christianity.]

> *"Higham argues compellingly that it had two purposes: to re-establish, contrary to Bede, the Britons as a people of the Lord in providential history, and to establish the primacy of the kings of Gwynedd among them."* [29]

The tract itself is easily documented and is fascinating in its extensive dichotomies from modern and standard Biblical accounts of creation and the flood.   The account of creation is essentially true to Biblical narratives. The descriptions of Heaven are profuse with images of precious stones and gold and the scale is precise *"ten times as large as the world."* The presence of a *"cross of gold on each door of those"* [30] in an old testament setting is anachronistic as is the description of the progression of man into heaven,

> *"...there goeth not into that city except one-third of the people of the world: namely, the person with the righteous gift of God and the pure person that kept his truth and the person of distinguished penance."* [31]

As in many of the other tracts in The Book of Lismore, order and structure is shown as crucial and

> *"Archangels with their troops are next to the Angels; Virtues are next to the Archangels; Powers are next to virtues; Principalities are next to powers..."* [32]

The fall of Lucifer is attributed directly to pride and his refusal to *"give reverence"* to Adam which in turn leads to the temptation of Adam and Eve. The creation of Adam and Eve is given in detail and we are again presented with the significance of the magical number nine:

> *"Nine months, indeed, from the time Adam received a soul until issued Eve from his side. And it is according to that precedent is every woman of her seed pregnant from that hither."* [33]

Conversion of images to local idiom is provided in the account of events following the fall when Adam and Eve conceal their nakedness not with fig leaves for *"there was not found in Paradise a tree upon which was foliage except the sycamore."* [34]

---

[29] Wiseman, Howard M. *The historicity and historiography of Arthur: A critical review of King Arthur: Myth making and history by N. Higham, and The reign of Arthur: From history to legend by C. Gidlow [in] The Heroic age: A journal of early medieval North-Western Europe.* 2007.

[30] MacCarthy, B. *The codex Palatino-Vaticanus No. 839 [Todd Lecture Series Vol. III] Ireland: Royal Irish Academy,* 1892 pg. Pg. 39.

[31] *Do. pg. 41.*

[32] *Do. pg. 43.*

[33] *Do. pg. 49.*

[34] *Do. pg. 57.*

The section following the fall is the most interesting part of the narrative as it deals with the travails of Adam and Eve outside paradise. Adam convinced that penance is essential decides on a prolonged period of immersion in the River Jordan by himself and instructs Eve to do likewise in the River Tigris where *"…be thy hair loosened upon every side upon the surface of the stream."* [35] This method of penitential expression was a central facet of Irish ascetic practice and occurs in many other sections of the Book of Lismore. An exploration of this theme has been made by Kay Muhr in *Celtica*. [36] Radner has also made significant reference to this in his article on historiography. Muhr adds that The Irish,

> *"seem to have felt most sympathy with the rural tribal society depicted in the opening books of the Old Testament, from Genesis to Kings."* [37]

Eve carries out Adam's wishes but is again tempted and falls prey to Lucifer. Satan subsequently informs Adam that he is being punished because he *"went against the will of my Lord, namely, Jesus Christ."* [38]

The account of the period leading to the flood is more fully explored in Lebor Gabála where we are informed,

> *"…for the Flood drowned the whole seed of Adam except Noah and his three sons, Shem, Ham, Japhet…We Gaedil are descended from Japhet."* [39]

The section also includes an important reference to the Antichrist.

What is particularly impressive in the tract are the layers of thought, sophistication of expression and parallel referencing: For instance in the Penance of Adam by immersion in the River Jordan we are presented with; a pre-figuring of the sacrament of baptism; the baptism of Christ in the same river; and the penitential power of the *"washing away of sins by water"*. The last point is particularly noteworthy as this theme is not only pervasive in Irish Christian literature but as has already been stated it regularly occurs in the Book of Lismore.

---

[35] *Do. pg. 65.*

[36] *Muhr, Kay. Water imagery in early Irish Ireland: Celtica 23 DIAS 1999 pgs. 193-210.*

[37] *Do. pg. 198.*

[38] *MacCarthy, B. The codex Palatino-Vaticanus No. 839 [Todd Lecture Series Vol. III] MacCarthy pg. 69.*

[39] *Lebor Gabála Érenn: The Book of the Taking of Ireland Part I pg. 1.*

A History of the Children of Israel

Unfortunately only a few short lines of this seminal piece have survived. Whitley Stokes in his Lives of Saints has provided a translation,

> *"For rather than that the Jews should be fed by it, they preferred that it should vanish, so they might die of hunger: for this was the desire of the Roman raiders, that all the Jews might die of hunger, for they were sorrowful at killing them..."* [40]

He also suggests that this section called *"Dígal fola Crist, 'Revenge for Christ's blood' 'is founded partly on Josephus account of the destruction of Jerusalem by Titus, and corresponds with the mediaeval French Vengeance du Sauveur."* [41] This view is endorsed by Macalister who in his analysis postulates with great conviction and gives telling arguments for the thesis that these two sections correspond directly to, and are copies of, parallel segments in An Leabhar Breac. In the absence of contrary views it is fair to describe and analyse the works of Josephus in the context of their probable presence in the Book of Lismore.

Josephus Flavius 37-100A.D. was a member of the Jewish religious and political elite. He became a Pharisee at 19 and has produced four major works: The Jewish War (first published 73A.D. then in extended form 75-79A.D.); Antiquitate Judaicae (in twenty books 93-94A.D.); Vita; and Contra or In Apionem [A validation of the antiquity of the Jews as a race].

His life corresponded with, and his work reflects, a period of *"cataclysmic transformation of the Jewish faith from a hierarchical cult based on animal sacrifice to a universal faith,"* and the birth of Christianity. His work serves to *"demonstrate the nature of classical literature"* and is particularly rich in its philology and grammar. He is a critical figure in the development of classical historiography and has directly stated his central objective,

> *"Surely to leave a permanent record of events not previously recorded for the benefit of posterity is worthy of the highest praise; and the real worker is not the man who merely changes the order and arrangement of another man's work, but the one who has something new to say and constructs a historical edifice of his own."* [42]

---

[40] Stokes, Whitley. Lives of Saints from the Book of Lismore Oxford: Clarendon Press, 1890 pg. VII.

[41] Stokes, Whitley. Lives of Saints from the Book of Lismore Oxford: Clarendon Press, 1890 pg. VI.

[42] Josephus. The Jewish war translated by G.A. Williamson revised with a new introduction, notes and appendices, by E. Mary Smallwood. U.K.: Penguin Books, 1981 511p. pg. 29.

In the Jewish War Josephus provides a terse account of the events while in Vita he is largely concerned with self-justification and explanation. The importance of the work is without doubt,

> *"The only other ancient military campaign that has been described in such detail by an eyewitness/participant is Julius Caesar's Gallic Wars."* [43]

and while Kenneth Atkinson has expressed considerable reservations on the accuracy of the account, *"the archaeological excavations and the topography of each site to suggest that he largely fabricated the basic details of these sieges"* [44] the history stands as a seminal study.

The Jewish War was originally written in Aramaic and subsequently translated into Greek in an extended version by the author. The prose is dense with graphic and powerful descriptive passages which sometimes descend into intermittent inane populist phraseology.

Having sketched the historical background Josephus proceeds to describe his early experiences of the war and his posting as a general to the area of Galilee. His description of the Roman Military formations and methods is extraordinarily detailed and complete. In his role, he served as commander of the city of Jotapata. He initially proved a capable and inventive leader as exemplified by his counter-siege strategies:

> *"He ordered the men to fix railings to the wall and over these to stretch raw oxhides, so that when the stones were hurled by the engines fell on them, they would give without splitting; other types of missiles would glance off them and firebrands would be quenched by their moisture."* [45]

However after his capture by the Romans and conversion to their cause he has been described as displaying *"despicable treachery."* Josephus then describes the events leading up to and including the siege of Jerusalem. His descriptions of the siege are unrelenting in their power and we are told that the besieged,

> *"showed no pity for grey hairs or helpless infancy, but picked up the children as they clung to their precious scraps and dashed them on the floor."* [46]

---

[43] *Do. pg. 1.*

[44] *Atkinson, Kenneth. "Noble deaths at Gamla and Masada?: A critical assessment of Josephus's accounts of Jewish resistance in light of archaeological discoveries" [in] Making History: Josephus and historical method (Supplements to the Journal for the study of Judaism) ed. by Zuleika Rogers. Netherlands: Brill, 2006 471p.*

[45] *Josephus. The Jewish war translated by G.A. Williamson revised with a new introduction, notes and appendices, by E. Mary Smallwood. U.K.: Penguin Books, 1981 511p. pg. 203.*

[46] *Do. pg. 324.*

To get food for themselves they had no compunction in using torture and *"stuffed bitter vetch up their genital passages and drove sharp stakes into their seats."* [47]   The horrors include a description of cannibalism by a mother on her child and the ramifications of the war are enormous, *"all the prisoners taken from the beginning to end of the war totalled 97,000; those who perished in the long siege 1,100000"* . [48]

The work concludes with a description of the destruction of Masada defended by the Sicarii and its famous suicide pact in which 960 perished from which only one old and one young woman together with *"five little children"* survived.

We are presented in the work with a portrait of Pontius Pilate who emerges as one of the early figure in the establishment of Roman power. He is shown to have had considerable difficulty with the Jews following his placement of imperial images throughout Palestine and in consequence,

> *"when Pilate visited Jerusalem they surrounded the tribunal and shouted him down. But he had foreseen this disturbance, and had made the soldiers mix with the mob…and the Jews were cudgelled, so that many of them died from the blows…"* [49]

The success of Josephus as a writer was immediate and lasting. He has provided us with *"the ultimate work for Judaism in the Greco-Roman period."* [50] And thanks to him we *"know more about Palestine in the first century A.D. than we do about any other part of the Roman Empire at that period – or indeed at many others"* [51] and

> *"In setting out to make the tragedy of his people known to the gentile world Josephus succeeded beyond his wildest dreams. His story has lived down the centuries as a treasured legacy from antiquity."* [52]

His reputation is enduring and in his book Louis Finkelstein quotes a lecture by Henry St. John Thackeray which fully endorses the position Josephus:

> *"There was a time in his country (England) when almost every house possessed two books, a bible and a Josephus in the old eighteenth-century version of William Whiston."* [53]

---

[47] *Do. pg. 324. There are some 140 species of the genus Vetch which is related to the lentil. It is recorded as being grown for over 9500 years and while the Bitter Vetch was consumed by humans for a period it was soon removed from the human staple. It is generally toxic to non-ruminants and can cause lathyrism.*

[48] *Do. pg. 371.*

[49] *Do. pg. 139.*

[50] *Mason, Steve. Josephus and the new testament [online article] pg. 1.*

[51] *Josephus. The Jewish war translated by G.A. Williamson revised with a new introduction, notes and appendices, by E. Mary Smallwood. U.K.: Penguin Books, 1981 511p. pg. 18-19.*

[52] *Do. pg. 24.*

[53] *Finkelstein, Louis. The Jews: Their history, culture and religion: U.S.: Harper & Brothers Publishers, 1949 pg. 754.*

The position of his work was enhanced by the light that it provided *"on the milieu of Jesus"* [54] and critically by the common interpretation of Jerusalem's fall as God's punishment which *"continued to flourish throughout the Middle Ages."* [55] His work provides the *"first reference outside new Testament"* to Christ who is mentioned in the Antiquities but not in Jewish War and while there are different versions of this reference, that provided in a 10th century Arab version is perhaps the most authentic,

> *"At this time there was a wise man who was called Jesus, and his conduct was good, and he was known to be virtuous. And many people from among the Jews and the other nations became his disciples. Pilate condemned him to be crucified and to die. And those who had become his disciples, did not abandon their loyalty to him. They reported that he had appeared to them three days after his crucifixion, and that he was alive. Accordingly they believed that he was the Messiah, concerning whom the Prophets have recounted wonders."*
> (Antiquities 18:63-64)

The testimony as quoted above was used by Eusebius in 324A.D. and so any changes could only have occurred between original publication and then. So central is this reference that *"for hundreds of years no work on the life of Jesus failed to refer to the Testimonium Flavianum (ant. XVIII, 63-64), Josephus' supposed eyewitness account of the Christian messiah."* [56]

In conclusion so central is the work of Josephus in describing this period that countless studies have been undertaken which

> *"could not have been written were it not for Josephus. Had his works perished, even such basic problems as describing the peoples of the land of Israel would remain unsolved. Josephus's writings are also crucial for the knowledge of the classical Greek and Roman traditions…"* [57]

It is obvious from a cursory study why such a seminal text would have been included in the Book of Lismore and it is unfortunate that the precise version has been lost as it would have provided for interesting comparative studies with the other classical pieces in the Book of Lismore.

---

[54] Bloom, James. Josephus as a source for a military history of the Jewish revolt. [online article] 2000 pg. 1.

[55] Do. pg. 2.

[56] Feldman, L.H. Josephus and modern scholarship (1937-1980) New York: Walter de Gruyter, 1984 1055p.

[57] Do. 1055p.

Section II

Lives of the Saints

This section contains biographies of nine Irish Saints: Patrick; Colum Cille; Brígid, Senan mac Geirrgin; Findian of Cluain Iraird; Finnchua of Brí Gobhain; Brenainn mac Finnloga; Ciarán of Clonmacnoise; and Mochua of Balla. The selection of some of the saints can be attributed to their recognized status but the rationale for the presence of others is unclear. A classic English translation was produced by Whitley Stokes [58] and is readily available today.

In reading the lives several interlinked themes and some interesting events emerge. In the life of Saint Patrick the origin of his enslavement is attributed not to Irish marauders but to the four sons of the King of Bretain [59] who have been in exile and having killed Patrick's parents *"They seized Patrick and his two sisters, even Lupait and Tigris….and they sold Patrick to Miliuc Maccu-Buain…and they sold Patrick's sisters in another quarter; and they (the children) knew nothing of each other."* [60] To Colomb Cille is attributed a miracle in the Island of Iona *"and he banished toads and snakes out of it."* [61]

The Life of St. Brigid is one of the more interesting and valuable of the hagiographies displaying in an intertwined way the merging of Druidic and Christian traditions and also the use of folklore phrasing and conventions. Prior to the birth of Brigid who's mother was bondmaid to her father the Druid says to Dubthach father of Brígid – *"Marvellous will be the child that is in her womb…The seed of thy wife will serve the seed of the bondmaid."* [62] Later we encounter the magical power of the Saint: *"Once upon a time Brigit had a band of reapers reaping. A rain-storm pours on the whole plain of Liffey, but not a drop fell on her field."* [63] This blending of traditions is also apparent in the life of Findian [Finen or Finnian] where while living in Wales he vanquishes the Saxons, *"Findian gave a blow of his staff on the mountain so that the mountain fell on the Saxons, and not a man of them escaped to tell the tale."* [64]

---

[58] *Lives of Saints from the Book of Lismore translated by Whitley Stokes Oxford: Clarendon Press, 1890.*

[59] *This was a part of southern England largely encompassing modern Devon and Cornwall.*

[60] *Lives of Saints from the Book of Lismore translated by Whitley Stokes Oxford: Clarendon Press, 1890 pg. 153 section 133.*

[61] *Lives of Saints from the Book of Lismore translated by Whitley Stokes Oxford: Clarendon Press, 1890. pg. 180 section 1070.*

[62] *Lives of Saints from the Book of Lismore translated by Whitley Stokes Oxford: Clarendon Press, 1890. pg. 183 section 1161.*

[63] *Pg. 197 section 1662.*

[64] *Pg. 224 section 2561.*

From a Waterford perspective the life of Brenainn or Brendan is the most important section. It highlight's the Irish tradition of fosterage *"At the end of a year then Bishop Eirc took him with him to his own foster-mother, even Íta, and Brenainn remained five years with Íta. And the nun gave him exceeding love, for she used to see the service of angels above him, and the grace of the Holy Spirit manifestly upon him; and it is thus that Brenainn used to be, calling continually to the nun whenever he would see her."* [65] It should be noted that St. Íta was a Princess of the Deisi who established a major monastery in Limerick. This reference in the Book of Lismore is one of the earliest and most important references to her status.

The importance and attribution of motivation to the travels of Brendan is most graphically set out *"Now after they had seen that paradise among the waves of the sea, they marvel and wonder greatly at the miracle of God and his power, and they greatly honour and glorify the Lord after seeing those mighty miracles."* [66]

In the story of St. Ciarán of Clonmacnoise we again see the marriage of pagan and Christian traditions *"On a certain day robbers came out of Offaly to kill people in the district of Cenél-Fiachrach, and they found the holy Ciarán with his herds, reading; and they proceeded to kill him. Howbeit they were stricken with blindness, and they could not put forth foot or hand till they made repentance; and then they were loosed by God's blessing and Ciarán's."* [67] Finally in the life of Mochua of Balla we see reflected the long Irish tradition of fertility and its symbols stretching back to the Silé na Gigs and here expressed in unequivocal terms *"A certain barren woman came onto him, and he blessed two sprigs of watercress for her, and she at once conceived a son and a daughter, to wit, Luicenchair the Pious and Scanlan were these."* [68]

Macalister in his introduction provides a valuable analytic note on the Lives,

> *"These Hagiographa,…should be described as 'homilies' rather than 'lives.' The difference lies herein, that with the former a biblical text is taken as a motto, and it is definitely stated or implied that the writing is meant to be read for the edification of the Faithful on the feast-day of the saint to which each is devoted. Thus the Patrick text is meant for a ceremony on 17 March; the Colum Cille for 9 June; the Brigid for 1 February; the Senan, for 22 February; the Ciarán for 9 September; and the Mochua for 27 March."* [69]

---

[65] *Pg. 249 section 3380.*

[66] *Pg 260 section 3873.*

[67] *Pg. 267 section 4090.*

[68] *Pg. 286 section 4787.*

[69] *The Book of Lismore. Introduction by R.A.S. Macalister Manuscripts Commission 1950 pg. xvii.*

Ríagal Phátraic

This is a crucial medieval text only a fragment of which has been preserved in the Book of Lismore but a much fuller rendition is provided in An Leabhar Breac. A translation of the fragment has been provided by Stokes in the Lives of Saints:

"Freeing of God's Church, with baptism and communion and chanting of requiems; with boys to read, with offerings of Christ's body upon every altar. It is not entitled to tithes, nor to a heriot cow, nor to an annoit's third, nor to…unless the proper reciprocal duties of the church (are performed) therein, (namely) of baptism and communion and chanting of requiems for her monks, both live and dead, and so that there be offering on the altar on Sundays and high-tides, and so that there be complete implements on every altar of them. No church that has not its proper (furniture) is entitled to the full fine of God's church, but its name is, according to Christ, a cave of thieves and robbers." [70]

The origins of the tract are somewhat uncertain but it appears most likely that it reflects, *"Patrick's support of the adoption of their own, pre-existing cultural institutions for Christian use, rather than his own personal involvement in the establishment of monastic communities"* [71] in Ireland. It is very possible that the invocation of the name of Patrick was applicable to the Ecclesiastical seat of Patrick in Armagh, the rationale for which was the application of authority to the tract.

In substance Ríagal Phátraic *"is an eight-century documents which, although entirely devoted to ecclesiastical matters, resembles a legal tract in style and content and is extant in its fullest recension in a manuscript containing other vernacular legal material."* [72] Before studying the content of the tract it is important to relate its rai-son d'ê-tre to the development of the early Irish church and particularly the popularity and nature of monasticism in the country. The establishment of early monastic and hermetic life was ascetic in form particularly in the Celtic church in Gaul as early as the 4th century. By the 6th century this model had been adopted in Ireland as major monastic growth occurred. In Europe, however, the monasteries tended to follow the Benedictine rule which was much less ascetic. In a critical point made by Margaret Lozano we are presented with a possible reason for this variation,

"Because of the lack of so-called 'red' martyrdom in Ireland, the Irish church placed a higher value on asceticism and missionary fervour, two qualities that, beginning with Patrick, came to represent the nature of Sainthood in Ireland." [73]

---

[70] Stokes, Whitley. *Lives of Saints from the Book of Lismore* Oxford: Clarendon Press, 1890 pg. 359.

[71] Lozano, Margaret. *Saint Patrick and the Irish Church.* [online article 2009] pg. 5.

[72] Etchingham, Colmán. *Church organisation in Ireland A.D. 650 to 1000* Ireland Laigin Publications, 1999 pg. 63.

[73] Lozano, Margaret. *Saint Patrick and the Irish Church.* [online article 2009] pg. 2.

While accepting that there is a lack of evidence for this conclusion she later quotes Ludwig Bieler that *"Patrick's ecclesiastical administration was based on a monastic framework."* [74] In the evolution of Ríagal Phátraic it would appear that the range and power of the monasteries was a critical component in the equation. In discussing the Church structure of the period Kathleen Hughes indicates the significance of the tract stressing that a system of reciprocal relationships is set out in two versions *"one incorporated into the Rule of the Célí Dé, the other known as Ríagal Phátraic"* [75]

Colmán Etchingham has provided an incisive and persuasive analysis of the piece in his seminal book *Church organisation in Ireland A.D. 650 to 1000* and it is largely from his work that the following observations have been gleaned.

Ríagal Phátraic belongs to a series of law tracts which are *"the largest body of prescriptions in Irish illustrative of ecclesiastical rulership."* Amongst other regulations it,

> *"provides for Episcopal supervision of pastoral ministration, apparently within a territorially defined sphere. Thus it is affirmed that there should be prímescop cecha túaithe 'a chief bishop of every lay community,' whose special function is to ordain clergy, consecrate churches and act as confessor do flaithib 7 airchindchib 'to lords and ecclesiastical heads' and whose unique power to provide the essential sacrament of confirmation is confirmed."* [76]

The emphasis in Ríagal Phátraic is to distinguish the roles of monastic and Episcopal clergy and it sets out the essential pastoral role of a Bishop. A critical element in the piece concerns levies to be made for clerical services and it is interesting to note that one consequence appears to have been that,

> *"burial of the general laity in ecclesiastical precincts, far from being normal, may well have been relatively unusual in the first millennium."* [77]

Commenting on Richard Sharpe's article *"Hiberno-Latin laicus, Irish láech and the Devil's men"* [in Ériu 30, pgs 75-92] Etchingham says that *"no other text deals exclusively with Episcopal supervision of the ministry and especially with its day-to-day conduct by the lower clergy."* [78]

---

[74] *Do. pg. 4.*

[75] *Hughes, Kathleen. The church in early Irish society. U.K.: Methuen & Co. Ltd., 1966 pg. 140.*

[76] *Etchingham, Colmán. Church organisation in Ireland A.D. 650 to 1000 Ireland Laigin Publications, 1999 pg. 63.*

[77] *Etchingham, Colmán. "Pastoral provision in the first millennium: a two-tier service? [in] The parish in Medieval and Early Modern Ireland: Community, Territory and Building. Edited by Elizabeth Fitzpatrick and Raymond Gillespie. Ireland: Four Courts Press, 2006 352p pg. 88.*

[78] *Etchingham, Colmán. Church organisation in Ireland A.D. 650 to 1000 Ireland Laigin Publications, 1999 pg. 239.*

In summary Ríagal Phátraic is a central tool in establishing and setting out church rules and obligations of flock and clergy and is rigid, technical, and bureaucratic in describing an almost feudal like inter-relationship structure.

In an article in *"The parish in medieval and early Modern Ireland"* Etchingham cites the view of D. Ó Coráin that the impact of Ríagal Phátraic *"is likely to have been restricted in practice to the particular dependants of the Church known as the manaig."* [79] In an historical contest, however, Ríagal Phátraic *"is a crucial text for all modern writers about the ministry."* [80]

Cosc Mo-C[h]olmoc meic ui Benna

Only the opening ten lines of this piece are provided and the extract ends precipitously.

As doilghi leam iná in t-éc [81]

This is a poem in eleven quatrains which would appear to have been included for primarily literary reasons.

---

[79] Etchingham, Colmán. *"Pastoral provision in the first millennium: a two-tier service? pg. 80.*

[80] *Do. pg. 83.*

[81] *The Book of Lismore. Introduction by R.A.S. Macalister Manuscripts Commission 1950 pg. xvii. Macalister provides an important note at this point: These three short pieces… [Riaghal Pátraic, Cosc & As doilghi] on the verso of folio 81, printed by Stokes without translation or comment in Lives of Saints, p. 135, are a Rule of Patrick relating to the exemption of religious houses from taxation, a series of short moral aphorisms attributed to a certain Mo-Cholmoc macu Benna, of whom I can find nothing further, and a pessimistic poem in eleven quatrains, anticipating a time of religious and moral apostasy at the end of the world."*

Section III

Anecdotes

This section contains thirteen anecdotes of which *"St Molaise and the nun"* is perhaps the most interesting.

Story of Three Young Clerics

This is a short piece concerning a voyage or pilgrimage taken by three young clerics. They had travelled to an island in search of monastic isolation, ascetic purity, fasting and a place of prayer. They had brought no provision *"save three cakes"* but their cat in catching a salmon challenged their purpose and increased their will to extend their ascetic endeavour.

They agree a priestly vow of prayer and a commitment that on the death of any of them those remaining would incorporate the vow of the man who had died. Eventually only one is left and he is forced to fulfil his colleagues vows for many years. His exertions eventually so overcome him that the

> *"thrice fifty psalms and the thrice fifty prayers and the thrice fifty Hymnum dicats, with the three masses every day and with celebration of the hours"* [82]

lead to his belief that the *"Lord hath a greater love for you twain than he hath for me."* But he is visited by an angel who informs him that because he undertook a more difficult mission he has lived the longest and will be rewarded with the kingdom of heaven. His acceptance is thereafter immediate and unequivocal and

> *"so he dwelt in his island till he was aged and withered, and till Brenainn came from the sea; and Brenainn blessed him and gave him communion and sacrifice so he went to heaven; and a watch of angels is always over them in their island."* [83]

As with the following piece we are assured that the power of prayer will overcome all challenges.

---

[82] Stokes, Whitley. *Lives of Saints from the Book of Lismore. Edited with a translation, notes and indices by Whitley Stokes. [Anecdota Oxoniensia]* Oxford: Clarendon Press, 1890. pg. IX.

[83] Stokes, Whitley. *Lives of Saints from the Book of Lismore. Edited with a translation, notes and indices by Whitley Stokes. [Anecdota Oxoniensia]* Oxford: Clarendon Press, 1890. pg. X.

St. Molaise and the Nun

This is a short story containing several of the themes of early hagiographies. The tale concerns an illicit relationship between a young nun and a clerical student. The nun had died in childbirth, is buried in a bog near the monastery of Molaise and is condemned to hell by the Saint. Her lover's prayers are so avid and pervasive that he secures her salvation and following her redemption *"Fursa the Pious"* extracts from Molaise her reburial in holy ground.

There are three central and related themes within the tale: Firstly we are presented with woman the temptress or a Molaise states *"a diabolic nun"*; Secondly we are persuaded of the importance of burial in holy ground; and finally and most crucially we are appraised of the power of prayer and specifically the fact that *"the Beatus is better than any prayer for saving a soul from devils."* [84]

Story of Two Young Clerics

This piece concerns the centrality of prayer in the ultimate objective of the achievement of everlasting life in heaven. As in *"Saint Molaise and the nun"* it specifically extols the *"Beatus."*

The story relates to two clerics who had been *"comrades since they had been little boys."* They made a pact that whosoever died first would return and *"bring tidings"* to the other of the nature of the next world. Following the death of the first cleric the other is not visited and:

> *"he was reproaching him and reproaching the Trinity for not letting him commune with him."* [85]

In his frustration he struck his head on a *"cross-beam so that he became dead."* In this state he incurs a phenomenon that has been described by many who have had a near death experience; that of floating above his own body. He is unaware that it is his body he is seeing and when *"the reapers"* come and place it in the local church he is unable to communicate with them. In the church he encounters his dead colleague and berates him for not having visited. The latter explains,

> *"I came many times, and was at the end of thy pillow complaining to thee; and thou heardest me not, for the thick, dense body heareth not the aerial attenuated soul."* [86]

---

[84] Stokes, Whitley. *Lives of Saints from the Book of Lismore. Edited with a translation, notes and indices by Whitley Stokes. [Anecdota Oxoniensia]* Oxford: Clarendon Press, 1890. pg. X.

[85] Stokes, Whitley. *Lives of Saints from the Book of Lismore. Edited with a translation, notes and indices by Whitley Stokes. [Anecdota Oxoniensia]* Oxford: Clarendon Press, 1890. pgs. xi-xii.

[86] Stokes, Whitley. *Lives of Saints from the Book of Lismore. Edited with a translation, notes and indices by Whitley Stokes. [Anecdota Oxoniensia]* Oxford: Clarendon Press, 1890. pg. xii.

Despite his earnest wish to remain the Cleric is forced to return to his body:

> "Truly thou shalt go, and thou wilt be a year alive, (Say) the Beatus every day for my soul, for the mightiest ladder and chain and collar to bring man's soul out of hell is the Beatus." [87]

The piece concludes with the death of the remaining Cleric and his elevation to heaven.

Brenuinn Maccu Altai and the Angel

This short piece expounds the superiority of the next world and extols the virtues of asceticism as a means of attaining it. A cleric at the monastery of Brennain had a wonderful gift for music and performance on the harp. He wished to play for Brennain but:

> "'He would not let you [come] to him' says the monks, 'for it is now seven years since Brennain smiled or heard a melody of the melodies of the world. But he has two waxen balls with a thread between them, and they used to lie before him on the book; and whenever he heard a melody he puts the balls into his ears'" [88]

However the cleric persisted with his intent and went to the Saint. After some difficulty the cleric achieved his aim and was blessed by the saint. Brennain explained that he had once been visited by "Michael the Angel" in the form of a resplendent bird who had played the most beautiful music for him. Brennain had subsequently made a vow to God that:

> "after that melody no melody of the world's melodies seems sweeter to me than this stole [?] over the neck, and to hear it I hold to be little profit." [89]

Three Saints in the House of Daithí the Presbyter

This is a brief anecdote, which relates the story of a visit by Saint Colm Cille, Saint Comgall and Saint Cainnech to the house of Daithí. Because of the time of their arrival they are given no food and the following day being Friday and a day of fast they have an extended fast period.

> "This obscure story is really a periphrastic explanation of what follows, where we read that each of the trio uttered an oracular quatrain – a 'trance-utterance', induced by the long fast – which dictated to each individually the course laid down for him…Daithí then came in and uttered a prophesy on the future fortunes of the monastery of each of the three, based on the amount which each had consumed". [90]

---

[87] Do. pg. XII.

[88] Stokes, Whitley. Lives of Saints from the Book of Lismore. Edited with a translation, notes and indices by Whitley Stokes. [Anecdota Oxoniensia] Oxford: Clarendon Press, 1890. pg. XIII.

[89] Stokes, Whitley. Lives of Saints from the Book of Lismore. Edited with a translation, notes and indices by Whitley Stokes. [Anecdota Oxoniensia] Oxford: Clarendon Press, 1890. pg. XV.

[90] The Book of Lismore. Introduction by R.A.S. Macalister Manuscripts Commission 1950 pg. xviii.

The influence of hunger in the invocation of a psychedelic state on the Saints is by no means accidental in the impact expressed.

St. Patrick at Temair

This tale according to Macalister may be an *"excerpt from a larger collection of anecdotes."* It gives us an account of a miracle performed by St. Patrick at Tara. Having been called upon to cure Lugaid son of the King, Loiguire mac Néill of an ailment he in fact contributes to his death. After Lugaid's death St Patrick proceeds to incessant prayer and finally through the intercession of Michael the Archangel Lugaid is brought back to life. Following his success Patrick,

> *"commanded that every one should set aside 'a tenth for the king of the Clouds and a morsel for Michael' at every meal"* [91]

The nomination of *"a tenth"* is surely not unrelated to the attribution of tithes.

Máel Póil of Cell Becáin and the Nun's Ghost

This can be considered a companion piece to *"Saint Molaise and the nun"* and the *"Story of two young clerics."* The main objective appears to be the promotion of the *"Beatus"* as the best prayer for salvation. This story begins,

> *"Máel Póil, grandson of Cinead, even the abbot of the monastery of Cell Becáin, was with another monk discussing astrology. Afterwards, as he slept, he saw coming towards him a gospel-nun who had died six days before that, and great plaining she had."* [92]

She chastises him for talking of astrology rather than praying for her. On his enquiry as to which prayer she would prefer she requests the Beatus as it is *"the most acceptable to God."*

Story of Guaire Aidne and the Two Saints at Inis Cealtra [93]

This short piece presents us with an interesting tableau of altruistic motivations and vehicular devices. It is originally to be found in the Book of the Dún Cow and the version in the Book of Lismore is essentially true to the original. The central characters are Guaire Aidne, King of Connaught; Saint Caimin; and Cuimmine Fota, Abbot and Bishop of Clonfert. Saint Caimin who died towards the middle of the 7th Century founded an abbey, which subsequently became known as *"Teampul Camin,"* on the Island of Inis Cealtra which is located in Lough Derg. Some remnants of Caimin's Church are extant today but these date from a later church of the 10th Century. Caimin was in fact a Prince and step-brother of Guaire.

---

[91] *The Book of Lismore. Introduction by R.A.S. Macalister Manuscripts Commission 1950 pg. xviii.*

[92] *Stokes, Whitley. Lives of Saints from the Book of Lismore. Edited with a translation, notes and indices by Whitley Stokes. [Anecdota Oxoniensia] Oxford: Clarendon Press, 1890. pg. xv.*

[93] *For further valuable information on Caimin and the Island of Inis Cealtra see the Clare County Library Website.*

This particular story may have originated in the County Clare area. During an encounter at a church on the Holy Island each of the characters proposes benevolent devices for communal enhancement. Guaire Aidne seeks to have the church filled with gold so that it can be distributed amongst the poor. Cuimmne Fota proposes that it should be replete with books to provide enlightenment and finally Saint Caimin suggests that it be filled with all the diseases and ills of the world that these would infect him. The motivation for Caimin's nomination is unclear but must reside in either asceticism or more probably a straightforward wish to *"take unto himself"* the sins and ills of the world.

Each of the characters is granted his wish but interestingly there is no concluding statement of morality or result.

Story of Mochuta or Raithen

This short extract is from the life of Saint Mochuta and will be of particular interest to the student of Waterford hagiography and ecclesiastical history. It details an anecdote which relates how Mochuta during meals at his monastery *"whenever his hands happened to touch any of the food, he would rub his hands on his shoes which he wore daily."* [94] He is later struck with a great desire to leave his monastery and proceed abroad. On a visit to Saint Comgall he removes his shoes and Comgall prays:

> *"'Come out, O devil' said he, 'from the shoe; thou shalt not carry off any more the spoil which thou didst find.'…the devil leaped out of the shoe…'it was lucky for thee, thy falling in with Comgall, O Mochuta, for I would not have allowed thee to be two nights in the same place, because of the unfair advantage which thou gavest thine own shoes over the shoes of the convent…and I found no other way of getting at thee but only this."*

In conclusion Comgall intones in verse:

> *"It is good for a clerk to reside in one place*
> *And attend the (canonical) hours.*
> *It is mocking devils that put*
> *The spirit of restlessness in a man."* [95]

The rationale for this piece resides in the nature of temptation and its consequences in sins of commission, omission or perhaps mischance. The central precept resides in the message that satisfaction and success in life resides in the acceptance of a settled environment and prayer, particularly where circumstances are clement.

---

[94] *Plummer, Charles. Bethada name nÉrenn: Lives of Irish Saints; edited from the original MSS, with introduction translations, notes, glossary and indexes by Charles Plummer. Section III Vol. II. Oxford, Clarendon Press, 1922. pgs. 301-302.*

[95] *Do. pgs. 301-302.*

Scéal ar Moling

Saint Moling was the second Bishop of Ferns and died in 696 A.D. He is a key figure in the hagiography of Wexford & Carlow and the town of Monamolin bears his name. This story concerns an encounter between the Saint and the devil. It is particularly interesting that the temptations proposed are not concerned with offerings but rather attempts by the Devil to cause Moling to carry out reprehensible actions in response to his goading.

The devil arrives clothed in regal apparel claiming to be Christ but his attire enables Moling to identify him for what he is as Christ would have arrived *"dressed as a leper."* Following several attempts to get Moling to respond the devil eventually seeks to get the saint to curse him as *"the venom and the hurt of the curse will be on the lips from which it will come."* This should be read in the context of the *"Curse"* which is a central device in both Irish civil and ecclesiastical tradition.

Eventually Moling suggests the Devil make a genuflexion to the Lord but the devil responds that *"I cannot bend forward for backwards are my knees."* This response has interesting parallels with the picture of the Antichrist painted elsewhere in the Book of Lismore.

Finally as the devil departs he recites a verse of eight stanzas in praise of God which is somewhat incongruous for such a speaker and commences as follows:

> *"He is pure gold, he is the sky around the sun,*
> *He is a vessel of silver with wine,*
> *He is an angel, he is holy wisdom,*
> *Whoso doth the will of the king."*

Cairpre Crom and Ciarán Mac in Tsaeir

This piece, which also occurs in the Book of Fermoy, concerns a legend of Cairpre King of Hy Maine in Connaught. He was *"son of Feradach, son of Lugaid, son of Dala, son of Bresal, son of Maine the Great."* He was an unjust and harsh King who,

> *"was doing abundant evils to every one. So he was murdered and beheaded. He was afterwards brought back to life by Ciarán, who replaced his head, but so unskilfully that Cairpre was nicknamed Crom"*, [96] an appellation that means the *"stooped."*

The piece is of particular interest as on his restoration to life Cairpre bestows some 17 townlands on Saint Ciarán. The bequest is described in detail and significant and valuable topographical information is provided on the lands in question. It could be suggested that this latter information is the central objective of the piece and that the *"tale"* is purely a vehicle for the conveyance of what might otherwise be a dull and lifeless listing of names and places.

---

[96] Stokes, Whitley. *Anecdota Oxoniensia Lives of the Saints from the Book of Lismore. Edited with a translation, notes and indices by Whitley Stokes.* Oxford: Clarendon Press, 1890. pgs. xvi-xvii.

Brenainn Mac Finnloga and Dobarchú

This piece is a short extract from the life of Saint Brendan. It details an incident in which Brendan had gone to reside at Dubh Daire in Thomond. When some of his oxen wandered into a meadow owned by Dobarchú the latter had them slaughtered. In a fit of pique the Saint cursed Dobarchú with transformation into an otter as suggested by his name. Dobarchú, subsequently on a visit to a nearby river, catches a fish and having eaten falls into the river while quenching his thirst and is duly changed into an otter. Later his son comes to the river and when about to repeat his father's actions is warned by the otter in a short verse:

> *"The fish that I ate quickly burned me;*
> *It is that which turned me senseless;*
> *Ill was my errand, and my journey wretched,*
> *Depart (thou) and Creda, Ó Cúcúan"* [97]

Dobarchú remains as an otter until his death. The moral of the tale is unclear unless it may concern the protection of Clerical power and property but it certainly illustrates well the most interesting morphology of many Irish personal names.

Baithin Mac Brenainn [98]

This is a very brief note on Baithin who was a first cousin of Colum Cille. It effectively states that his entire life was spent in prayer for he:

> *"at no time, save the time of sleep only, was without doing some work for God, either praying,*
> *or reading, or writing, or humble service."*

---

[97] Plummer, Charles. *Bethada name nÉrenn: Lives of Irish Saints; edited from the original MSS, with introduction translations, notes, glossary and indexes by Charles Plummer. Section III Vol. II. Oxford, Clarendon Press, 1922.* pgs. 79-80.

[98] *Baithin mac Brenainn translated by Kuno Meyer. The Gaelic Journal Vol. IV No. 47* pg. 229.

Section IV

The ever-new tongue

This section contains an Apocryphon. The word has as its origin *"hidden,"* but over time evolved to *"comporting both want of genuineness and canonicity."* However, in this context it refers to apocryphal gospels *"which in the main seem to have been either embodiments of primitive tradition, or a mere recasting of canonical Gospels with a few variations and amplifications."* These literary pieces frequently attempted to cast further light on the unknown lives of St. Joseph, The Virgin Mary and Jesus Christ by *"inventing"* further accounts of events.

Whitley Stokes in his version and commentary originally published in 1905 has again provided us with an excellent study. [99] He indicates that this work is extremely rare and informs us that with some notable exceptions including the setting out the nine ranks of the celestial hierarchy the *"folklore in it is found in no other Irish composition."* [100] The Lismore text is *"difficult"* and he suggests that it *"may safely be ascribed to the tenth or eleventh century, when Old Irish was merging into the Early-Modern Irish of the Book of the Dun and the Book of Leinster."* [101] While acknowledging the uncertain source of the tract Stokes suggests *"that it may be a version of a lost Latin Apocalypse of Philip…"* [102]

The work entitled *"Tenga Bithnua"* or the *"Ever-new Tongue,"* takes the form of a *"dialogue between the Hebrew sages, assembled on Mount Zion on Easter-eve, and the spirit of the apostle Philip, who is called by the household of 'Ever-new Tongue,' because, when he was preaching to the heathen, his tongue was nine times cut out and nine times miraculously restored."* [103] It deals with the biblical events of the Books of Genesis and the Apocalypse.

The work displays affinities with Celtic mythologies at its inception:

> *"Nine times hath my tongue been cut out of my head by the heathen, and nine times I continued to preach again."* [104]

---

[99] *The Ever-new Tongue by Whitley Stokes. Ériu: The journal of the School of Irish Learning, Dublin. Vol. II, 1905 pgs. 96-163 pg. 96.*

[100] *Do. pg. 96.*

[101] *Do. pg. 97.*

[102] *Do. pg. 96.*

[103] *Do. pg. 96.*

[104] *Do. pg. 103.*

We are introduced to the theme of genesis and the generation of order by the works of God. This central theme exploring the nature of the deity who is eternal, unchanging is intriguing and very well expressed in the following extract:

> *"For 'tis in circularity of roundness the heavens have been made round about, and in circularity the seven seas have been made. And in circularity of roundness the stars traverse the round wheel of the universe, and in roundness of form the souls are seen after issuing from their bodies."* [105]

In dealing with the creation of the seas and oceans and in particular the 'flamy sea' we are again reminded of Celtic origins *"Out of the heavens are let nine winds which arouse (?) it from its sleep."* [106] In describing the stone of Adamant [diamond] which nothing can break or damage except the *"Blood of the Lamb of God"* we are as Stokes has confirmed [107] seeing a Christian modification of a myth described by Pliny.

In a section dealing with the creation of the birds we are introduced to a piece which has evoked much response:

> *"A bird of enormous size named Hiruath, is in the lands of India. Such is the size of its form that the shadow of its wings, when it expands them, extends to a journey of three winter-days by sea or lands."* [108]

The listeners are specifically advised to believe in the miracles of God and in a study on this section [109] Martin McNamara has explored possible links to Judaic traditions and the travels of Sinbad but comes to no definitive conclusions. There are echoes of the Amazonians in the section on the tribes of Creation as the women from the mountains of *"Armenia…bring forth daughters only."* [110] We are also provided with progressive poetic repetitive numbering *"two and seventy flocks of birds…two and seventy kinships of snakes."* [111]

---

[105] *Do. pg. 107.*

[106] *Do. pg. 113.*

[107] *Notes on The Ever-new Tongue by Whitley Stokes. Ériu: The journal of the School of Irish Learning, Dublin. Vol. III, 1907 pgs. 34-35.*

[108] *The Ever-new Tongue by Whitley Stokes. Ériu: The journal of the School of Irish Learning, Dublin. Vol. II, 1905 pgs. 96-163 pg. 121.*

[109] *The Bird Hiruath of the "Ever-new Tongue' and Hirodius of Gloss on PS. 103: 17 in Vatican Codex Pal. Lat. 68 by Martin McNamara. Ériu: The journal of the School of Irish Learning, Dublin. Vol. XXXIX. 1988. pgs. 88-94.*

[110] *The Ever-new Tongue by Whitley Stokes. Ériu: The journal of the School of Irish Learning, Dublin. Vol. II, 1905 pgs. 96-163 pg. 131.*

[111] *Do. pg. 133.*

Moving to the apocalyptical description of hell we are told that it is a place of *"all the kinds of monsters for mangling the souls in hell."* [112] It has fire, cold, darkness, stench, hunger, thirst, fear, grief, sorrow and sadness to assault the senses of the damned. The Day of Judgement will arrive as a fiery tempest with *"the coming of the nine ranks of heaven…"* [113] Stokes in his footnote describes these nine ranks of angels - *"They are, according to the pseudo-Dionysius the Areopagite – Thrones, Seraphim, Cherubim: Dominions, Authorities, Powers: Principalities, Archangels, Angels.."* [114]

Finally as the piece ends with the departure of the Ever-new Tongue we are informed that *"everything that had been said to them was written down by them. And that instruction which the Evernew Tongue gave was the beginning of the Faith."* [115]

---

[112] *Do. pg. 135.*

[113] *Do. pg. 139.*

[114] *Do. pg. 162.*

[115] *Do. pg. 147.*

This section is devoted to religious poems of which there are four:

Ocht N-Aerich na Ndualuch don Roichit for Rith
Ocht N-Aerich na Colnaidí

These first two poems in this section concern the *"Eight Capital Vices."* The first in supplied in a metrical style attributed to Máol-Ísa Ua Brolcháin [ob. 1088]. The second which is perhaps the more relevant and valuable forms part of a Colloquy of Colman and is also included in Agallamh na Senórach.

The origin of the nomination of Eight Capital Vices lies in an early Book of the Bible. In the Book of Proverbs we are presented with the *"six things the Lord hateth, and the seventh His soul detesteth."* Later in the Epistle to the Galatians we are provided with another but substantially different and longer list. However it was Evagrius Ponticus [346-399 A.D.], a deacon of Constantinople who in his treatise *"On the Eight Evil Thoughts"* provides a list: *"gluttony; fornication; avarice; dejection or lack of pleasure; anger; weariness or acedia; vainglory; and pride."* A Monk John Cassian [c.360-435] essentially restates the list of Evagrius. Pope Gregory the Great was the first to formulate a revised list as the *"Seven deadly sins."*

John Climacus later in the 7th century in his The Ladder of Divine Ascent presents a formula for victory over the eight thoughts. But a crucial and seminal evolution of the importance and popularity of the contest between the *"seven deadly sins"* and its contrasted virtues is provided by Dante Alighieri [1265-1321]. In his great work the Divine Comedy [begun 1308] he explores and extends this theme into a version which *"became perhaps the best known source since the Renaissance."*

William Langland [c.1332-1386] in his Vision of Piers Plowman; John Gower [1330-1408] in his Confessio Amantis; and Geoffrey Chaucer [c.1340-1400] in his Canterbury Tales, specifically the Parson's Tale which has as a central theme the seven deadly sins, provide further evidence of the extensive medieval interest in this theme.

The first poem in the Book of Lismore begins:

> *"The eight chiefs of the vices*
> *Which come to us speedily*
> *Against the virtues*
> *To expel them from the world."* [116]

---

[116] *Lives of Saints from the Book of Lismore translated by Whitley Stokes Oxford: Clarendon Press, 1890 pg. xviii.*

But it is in the second poem that we are provided with a more precise indication of the importance of the poems. In it we are given context through the dialogue between Colman and Caeilte with further links to Fianna and Celtic scene. Following the discovery of an antler and its deposit with Eochaid King of Ulidia, Colman relates the *"reason of the eight Hours"* to Caeilte. They purge the eight faults:

> *"The eight carnal imperfections, that gnaw us to the bone; the eight choice Hours, that vehemently banish them: Prime, against immoderate gluttony; Tierce, against anger born of many causes; cheerful lightsome Noon we constantly oppose to lust; Nones against covetousness so long as we are on the breast of weary Earth; pleasant and profitable Vespers we oppose to sore despair; Compline, against perverting weariness: this is a fair partition; cold Nocturns that equally divide [the night], against inordinate boasting [i.e. pride]; Matins of God's atoning Son, against enslaving sullen pride. Mayest thou, O judicial King, O Jesus, save me for the sake of the eight!"* [117]

This piece is followed by story of Ossian related by Caeilte.

Modern Catholic usage relates the sins as: pride, avarice, envy, wrath, lust, gluttony and sloth/acedia. Crucially pride is considered *"the original and most serious of the seven deadly sins, and indeed the ultimate source from which the others arise…"* and this emphasis can be seen in an early Irish context in the first section of the Book of Lismore where the sin of Lucifer is specifically outlined as that of pride.

It is of note that while these two poems are concerned with the *"eight capital vices"* in the wider church by this time these had been replaced by the *"seven deadly sins."* While the quality of the poetry may to some extent explain their presence in the Book it is also probable that their inclusion reflects deep thematic concerns and interests of the Irish church.

A Poem on the Day of Judgment

According to J.G. O'Keeffe this poem is *"possibly as old as the tenth century,"* [118] a proposition which he attributes to its metrical structure. Like many of the old Celtic pieces it possesses a raw earthiness and Rabelaisian [119] quality perhaps best known by most readers as in the very much later *"Midnight Court"* of Merriman.

---

[117] *O'Grady S.H. Translation [in] Silva Gadelica Vol. I pgs. 176-178.*

[118] *A poem on the day of judgment. Translated by J.G. O'Keeffe. Ériu: The Journal of the school of Irish Learning, Dublin. Ireland: Royal Irish Academy, 1976 [originally published 1907] pgs. 29-33.*

[119] *Francois Rabelais, 1494-1553.*

After two brief verses which set the scene the author rapidly gets to the core of his setting:

> *"When the earth will vomit forth the hosts of Adam's vast seed, when one blaze will fill both heaven and earth."*

He proceeds to deal with the evil and the good and issues a warning to those of his own day:

> *"The red-mouthed brehons, the lewd, the sinful, the satirists the contentious, arrogant clerics will find neither honour nor welcome."*

Following a succession of verses detailing the horrors of hell we are given a series of psalm like prayers for redemption and victory and triumph *"in the rout of Doom."*

Mithid Dhamsa Toirired

This is a short poem in ten quatrains which appears to have been included for literary rather than other reasons. The version in the Book of Lismore has been badly damaged but an alternative version is ascribed by Stokes to Saint Columcille while Macalister indicates that,

> *"In the Annals of the Four Masters, II A.D. 926, it is ascribed to Céle Dabhaill mac Scannláin, composed on setting out on his pilgrimage to Rome from Bangor."* [120]

Whitley Stokes provides a translation of the first four lines,

> *"Time for me to journey,*
> *To travel from Torach of (the) household,*
> *To go like a pilgrim*
> *Over a noble wave of t(the) joyful sea."* [121]

which would appear to confirm the theme of the poem. This piece located in a section where the earlier poems are centrally concerned with aspects of *"sin"* might be seen to suggest and validate the importance of pilgrimage as a suitable antidote or penance.

---

[120] *The Book of Lismore. Introduction by R.A.S. Macalister Manuscripts Commission 1950 pg. xx.*

[121] *Lives of Saints from the Book of Lismore translated by Whitley Stokes Oxford: Clarendon Press, 1890 pg. xviii.*

Section VI

The conquests of Charlemagne

This section portrays the life of Charlemagne the first Holy Roman Emperor who was born in 742 and died in 814. His capital was Aachen from where he ruled much of Western Europe. This extract deals in particular with his wars in Spain against the Saracen and Moorish invaders. His reign was instrumental in restoring some semblance of *"civilization"* in the wake of the collapse of the Roman Empire. One of his more interesting innovations was the introduction of the tithe or tenth part of the produce of the land as a means of Church support. An extremely accurate and readable version of the extract in the Book of Lismore has been provided by Douglas Hyde who translated this largely late-middle or early modern Irish version of the 14th or 15th century which was taken directly from the Latin original ascribed to Bishop Turpin, Archbishop of Rheims, 753-800 A.D.

Hyde indicates that this work is not that of Turpin *"but the work of different people writing at different times between the beginning of the eleventh and the middle of the twelfth century."* [122]   While using three early Irish mss, that in the Book of Lismore is his main source. He suggests that the dates of the original translations are difficult to determine and the variations are so considerable that they *"show that a long time must have elapsed and very many copies made from the original translation before they were themselves written."* [123]   However he states that the similarities in the three versions suggest that all were made from the same original translation and were taken from the Latin and not the French version. He thinks that the original translation was produced circa 1400 and points out that *"Of the three full copies at my disposal the copy in the Book of Lismore was made by the most literate, and the Egerton copy by the most illiterate of the scribes."* [124]

Within the body of the text one can identify many preoccupations of the period when the text was written. The motivation of the crusades is obvious in the phrase *"saved them from the hands of the Saracens."* [125]

---

[122] *Gabháltus Searluis Mháir. edited from the Book of Lismore and three other vellum mss. By Douglas Hyde. London: Irish Texts Society 1917. pg. vi.*

[123] *Do. pg. xi.*

[124] *Do. pg. xv.*

[125] *Do. pg. 3.*

However the romanticism and the conventions of the *"morality play"* emerge later as in an incident depicting the death of Charlemagne's champion Romaruicus who in death asks a friend to sell his horse and donate the proceeds in alms. This he fails to do and the dead Knight reappears to the miscreant and in an exact parallel to the ethic portrayed in Marco Polo states *"And since thou has unjustly kept back my alms to thyself, understand that thou hast kept me thirty days in pain, and be it known to thee that for that reason thou thyself shalt go to-morrow into hell, and that I shall go into Paradise."* [126] This message is repeated, as in the classic morality play, towards the end of the chapter *"unless he gives that alms he is himself damned."* [127]

The parallel with Polo and with preoccupations portrayed throughout the Book of Lismore are emphasised in attempts by Agiolandus, who on seeing his soldiers defeated and killed, made divinations with spells. The extreme didactic nature of the piece is emphasised again and again: *"And as Charles's knights prepared their weapons to fight, in such wise ought we to prepare our own arms to fight, namely good virtues to set against faults."* [128] *"and as Charles warred against Agiolandus on behalf of the Christian faith, and as he slew him, so it is obvious that the law of the Christians goes beyond each and every law, et cetera."* [129]

But, perhaps the most interesting and relevant piece in this entire section concerns the portrayal of a battle when Saracens come out with masks dreadful like devils and huge noise, *"so soon as the horses of the Christians heard the voices and sounds and noises of those trappings of wizardry, and beheld those awful appearances, great terror and horror seized them, and they turned back as though they were distraught or mad, and the knights could not keep them or hold them in at all. And when the other two bands of the Christians saw the first band fleeing towards them, they themselves, the whole of them, fled with them….Charles taking counsel ordered his fighting men to over the heads of their horses with cloths, so that they might not see the awful tricks which the Pagans had performed the day before. And he gave orders to stop the ears of the horses so that they might not hear the dreadful noises of the tabors or their [other] marvellous arts."* [130] This incident is directly parallel to an event mentioned in Marco Polo to which I will refer later and reminds me forcefully of an incident from the life of George S. Patton when following his first successful engagement against Erwin Rommel in the Desert War refers to Rommel's book *"The tank in attack"* and with inimitable fashion in deep elation intones *"Rommel you magnificent bastard I've read your book."*

---

[126] *Do. pg. 15.*

[127] *Do. pg. 17.*

[128] *Do. pg. 21.*

[129] *Do. pg. 45.*

[130] *Do. pgs. 65-67.*

The morality and ethics of this piece are further emphasised when following an engagement in which Christian knights *"lie with women"* are subsequently defeated but those who had not sinned were also lost and the reason given is prophetic in that the lord will *"grant them a crown in the kingdom of God."* [131] The writer further intones: *"Hence it is not a right or advantageous thing for women to be in the camps for luxurious-indulgence brings hindrance in their operations to both body and soul."* [132]

The rectitude of the Christian cause and the linkage between pre-Christian sorcery and Christian miracles is emphasised when subsequent to the death of Charlemagne areas are re-won by the Saracens and as they come to the Church of St James and try to remove decorative and rich pillars *"the man who was striking them, it came to pass by God's help when he thought to destroy the church, that that person became a stone, and that stone is ever since in that same church in the similitude of a man, and the like colour that was at that time on a Saracen's garments is on it now."* [133]

In conclusion this account contains both elements of ethical and moral education for the reader but has also within it, suggestions of military strategy to inform, and romantic heroism to edify the reader.

---

[131] *Do. pg. 81.*

[132] *Do. pg. 81.*

[133] *Do. pg. 115.*

Section VII

Anecdotes

This section contains a series of anecdotes including the notable and interesting *"The story of All Saints' Day."*

Scéal na Samhna: The Story of All Saints Day

This is a singularly important piece as it reflects the strategy of the early church to convert or incorporate established pagan places, buildings and festivals into Christian structures. In this case the conversion was not only of a place, The Pantheon, but also an occasion, the very important Festival of Samhna.

We are told that Pope Boniface IV in 609 A.D. petitioned the Emperor Phocas for the conversion of the Pantheon to Christian purposes. [134] This transfer was to be solemnised on the Feast of Samhna,

> *"This was right, for the Samain was the chief solemnity of the heathen at that time, for all the gods of the world, from east to west, were worshipped on that day."* [135]

Following the transfer, Boniface had the Pantheon rededicated to *"All Saints."* In a further tale narrated in the Book of Lismore we are informed that,

> *"The boys of Rome, says the story, traditionally played a game every year on this day. It was a board game with the figure of a hag at one end and the figure of a maiden at the other. The hag let loose a dragon against he opponent, while the maiden let loose a lamb. The lamb overcame the dragon. Then the hag sent a lion against the maiden, who caused a shower of hail which defeated it. Pope Boniface asked why the boys played this game and who had taught them. They replied that the Sibyl [136] taught them, in token of Christ's combat with the devil. The pope then forbade the game, since Christ's coming was a historical fact."*

In the context of the Celtic Festival it is critical to understand that the year was divided into two parts winter and summer and that The Feast of Samhna marked the start of the new year and *"was a day of changes, of births and deaths; it was an open door between the real world and the otherworld."* [137]

---

[134] *Interestingly this conversion may have been directly responsible for the preservation of the building following the collapse of the Roman Empire. The Pantheon had been built circa 25 B.C. and had been dedicated to Jupiter, Mars and Venus.*

[135] *Stokes, Whitley. Lives of Saints from the Book of Lismore. Edited with a translation, notes and indices by Whitley Stokes. [Anecdota Oxoniensia] Oxford: Clarendon Press, 1890. pg. xix.*

[136] *The Sibyls were any of several women priestesses of shrines, especially those of Apollo, as at Delphi or Cumae, who were inspired by the Gods to foretell future events.*

[137] *Early Irish myths and sagas. Translated with an introduction and notes by Jeffrey Gantz. Penguin Books, 1981 vi, 280p. pg. 12.*

Quoting Proinsias Mac Cana, Gantz indicates that the Festival marked a *"partial return to primordial chaos…the appropriate setting for myths which symbolise the dissolution of established order as a prelude to its recreation in a new period of time."* [138]

Scéal Ainnte Crisd: The Story of Antichrist [139]

This should be considered as a companion piece to *"The Ever-new tongue"* and will be of *"interest to the student of Apocryphal literature."* According to Douglas Hyde the features of the devil in this tract *"reminds one of the mediaeval idea of the Devil."* *"Antichrist"* may originate in the obvious term *"against,"* alternatively it may find derivation as *"one resembling Christ in appearance"* [140] and actions.

The Antichrist will be born of a *"harlot of the tribe of Bethel"* and *"and he will say that it is he who has always been commonly prophesied about."* [141] In size:

> *"the length of his body shall be six hundred fathoms, and forty fathoms in breadth, and one eye protruding from his 'forehead'…he shall have no knees, and the soles of his feet shall be round like the wheel of a cart, and there shall be horrible black hair on him…"* [142]

Those who support him will be branded with a hot iron and those who oppose him will be slain and *"he shall awaken the dead in imitation of Christ."* The world will become an intensely evil place and women *"shall have no shame, and they shall not conceal their shame nor their nakedness."* [143] The prophets Elias and Enoch will return from the dead to fight him but after *"two score and three hundred days fighting"* they will be defeated and killed but will subsequently be raised by God to *"eternal life."* The Archangel Michael will be sent to fight and *"he shall slay Antichrist with one blow."* *"And it is then that every Pagan and Jew and Gentile shall turn to the Catholic faith, and there shall be only three years and a half after that to the Day of Judgment"* [144]

---

[138] *Do. pg. 13.*

[139] *Mediaeval account of Antichrist: translated and edited by Douglas Hyde. Medieval Studies in Memory of Gertrude Schoepperle Loomis. 1927 pgs. 391-398.*

[140] *Do. pg. 393.*

[141] *Do. pg. 395.*

[142] *Do. pg. 396.*

[143] *Do. pg. 397.*

[144] *Do. pg. 398.*

The presence of this powerful, graphic and indeed *"hideous"* descriptive piece is one of the highlights of the entire Book. The concept of the Antichrist apparently predates not only the birth of Christianity but also that of Judaism. According to Timothy Perenich the concept,

> *"seems to have had its origin in Persian eschatology, where the battle between Ahura Mazda, the god of light, and Angra Mainyu, the god of darkness, plays a predominant role. And from there it found its way into Jewish apocalyptic literature, where the opposition between God and the devil, who is introduced under the various names of Beliar, Satanas, Diabolus, Pneuma-aerion..."* [145]

What makes the presence of this tract in the Book of Lismore so remarkable and so important is that accounts of, or references to, the Antichrist were by no means numerous during the medieval period.

Scéal ar Cainnech Naomh: A Story of Saint Cainnech

This is a most curious anecdote. It relates a story of Cainnech who while based at Roscrea sees a host of demons in the sky, one of whom descends to him. The demon informs Cainnech that they have come from the north of Connaught,

> *"to visit a friend and servant of theirs named Crom Dubh, and to give him the reward for his many misdeeds."* [146]

The rationale and scope of the tale is unexplained and its inclusion in the Book of Lismore is unusual.

Le Roi David & Le Mendiant

This is a short biblical tract relating to the lives of King David and his son Solomon. Critically, we are presented in the very first paragraph with an indication of the underlying theme of the piece:

> *"On Passover-day it was that to the poor and needy of the Lord David son of Jesse was used to distribute the tenth part of his substance, which process, once begun, had then become an appointed thing with them."* [147]

---

[145] Perenich, Timothy *Antichrist: From Persian dualism to contemporary Christianity. [online article] January 2009.*

[146] *The Book of Lismore. Introduction by R.A.S. Macalister Manuscripts Commission 1950 pg. xx.*

[147] O'Grady, Standish H. *Le Roi David & Le Mendiant [from] Mélusine, IV (1889), col. 163-6 pg. 164-164.*

The story concerns an able bodied mendicant who sought alms from King David and was advised to desist from further requests but continued to do so. David finally frustrated by the flouting of his authority ordered the mendicant hanged for his persistence but Solomon made an intercession on his behalf *"it were fitter to give him something."* [148] The king reluctant to alter his decision is persuaded by Solomon to give the beggar a blessing as he also does himself. The blessings are conveyed *"into his bosom"* and the beggar returned home to his wife and family. On his return, the beggar's cloak is washed in the river and from,

> *"every drop of water that with the current flowed through the rag was converted into a salmon, a veritable fish, to such a pitch that with the dint of salmon they could not in the river rinse about the old mantle."* [149]

The cloth is afterwards placed upon an apple tree which brought forth a great bounty of fruit and later three golden apples, *"each apple of them greater then the biggest head in the country."* These apples the now rich mendicant brought to King David and in a summation we are informed that *"treasure should be thus divided, viz. a third to the church; a third to the People and a third to the Prince."* [150]

The essence of the story deals unequivocally with the allocation of contributions to the church and the King. There is an underlying message that such alms will multiply to the benefit of the donor. The piece contains a fascinating and anachronistic reference to Jesus in which we are informed that as Solomon had been told by Christ that *"whatsoever he should ask of Him he should have."* Equally interesting are the central references to the *"salmon,"* as a source of wealth and bounty. These are at odds with the natural history of the Middle East and obviously have been chosen as imagery certain to be comprehended and appreciated by Irish readers.

Another Story of David

This piece, which begins *"No bid di(du) D(aui)d oc breith na hoeinbreithe cor int shamlai,"* is directly related to the preceding piece. It lacks obvious penetrative or obvious rationale for inclusion. The narrative concerns *"Solomon's impatience at the slowness of David's pronouncing judgements."* [151] One possible explanation would link the story to the importance of 'judgement' in the context of the Brehon Laws.

---

[148] *Do. pgs. 164-165.*

[149] *Do. pg. 165.*

[150] *Do. pg. 166.*

[151] *The Book of Lismore. Introduction by R.A.S. Macalister Manuscripts Commission 1950 pg. xxi.*

Sgél an Dá Leanabh

This is a simple story set in France concerning a visit by two children, one a Christian the other a Jew, to a church. On viewing and seeking an explanation of the religious iconography the Jewish child is informed by his companion of his race's culpability in the death of Christ.

"...it was thy people that crucified him, out of hatred and envy." [152]

The pair later have communion, and by inference the Jewish child is converted to Christianity. On his return home the Jewish child's parents are so angered by what has happened that they declare,

"'Thou art a criminal deserving of death, O son!' say they; and he is taken (by them and cast into) a furnace of the fire flaming redly, and he remained therein from the one watch to the other, so that dust and ashes were made of him." [153]

However. on opening the furnace the child is unscathed and attributes his safety to the Virgin Mary and so impressed are the parents that the too are converted. There is a palpable anti-Semitic tone in the phraseology and the message and in essence the piece appears to offer little beyond its obvious intent as a tool for the conversion of the *"infidels."*

Comgall of Bennchor [154]

This is a very short note concerning a competition in prayer and asceticism precipitated by a visit by a *"pious monk"* to Comgall of Bangor. Following various prayer vigils Comgall repairs into a river to recite the psalms and the pious monk follows but is unable to endure the heat and the cold and hence, *"he was not able to compete in devotion with Comgall."*

---

[152] *Stokes, Whitley. Lives of the Saints from the Book of Lismore. Oxford Clarendon Press. Pg. xxi.*

[153] *Do. pg. xxi.*

[154] *Comgall of Bennchor. Translated by Kuno Meyer. The Gaelic Journal Vol. IV No. 47 pg. 229.*

Section VIII

A history of the Lombards

According to Whitley Stokes this section is based on *"Historia gentis Langobardorum"* written by Paul the Deacon [720-799AD] a Benedictine Monk who was himself a member of a prominent Lombard Family born at Friuli. His literary skills earned him a place at the court of Charlemagne and he became a major figure in the Carolinian literary renaissance.

This piece narrates the history of the Langobards or Lombards from 568 to the death of King Lieutprand in 747. It is a major source for the history of the decline of the Roman Empire and contains much information about the Byzantine Empire, the rise of the Franks and the history of many of the other Barbarian Tribes. This history was written subsequent to the return of Paul the Deacon to Monte Cassino in 787 and the period up to his death. The source I have used here is an electronic online version. [155] The work is divided into six books of unequal extent.

Book I

In book I the author deals with the origin of the Langobards. Paul informs us that they *"came from an island which is called Scadinavia."* Berthold Schmidt [156] in his review:

> *"concludes that the word refers to the Scandinavian peninsula which was then considered an island; but he rejects the tradition that the Langobards actually migrated from Sweden to Germany, since he considered that they belonged to the West-German stock."* [157]

Paul suggests the population increase was decisive in the migrations and that the tribe divided into three parts and the progress of that part which ended in Italy is set out:

> *"The Winnili then, having departed from Scandinavia with their leaders Ibor and Aio, and coming into the region which is called Scoringa..."* [158]

We are informed that this took place circa in the 5th or 6th year of the Christian era during the reign of Caesar Augustus. We are given several possible sources for their name: Longbeards; Barta or an axe; Bord as in sea-board, from meadows near the Elbe; and finally from their worship of Wotten who bore the name *"long-bearded or grey-bearded."*

---

[155] Historia Langobardorum used text at www.northverg.org/lore/langobard/oo1.php. 6 books pagination non-sequential so quoting Book and chapter number only.

[156] Schmidt, Berthold. Die spate Völkerwanderungszeit in Mitteldeutschland...Mit einem anthropologischen. Berlin: Deutscher Verlag der Wissenschafter, 1976. 392p. [The late migration of people in Central Germany].

[157] Historia Langobardorum chapter II.

[158] Do. Chapter VII – Scoringa is described as being near the Elbe and about 24 miles south east of Hamburg.

Paul recounts the story of battle where to swell the impression of numbers women put hair in front of them like beards and opposition asked *"who are those Long-beards?"* But he discounts this story.

He develops the theme that with the Franks the Langobards were the only tribes to give conquered peoples emancipation and incorporate them into their forces thus becoming stronger and this contributed to their success when they arrived in Italy later. After a sojourn in Rugiland on the north side of Danube circa 65 A.D. there is little mention of them for over 300 years. Around 565 king Audoin led the Langobards to Pannonia [159] and later took over the city of Sirmium. [160]   During their time in Pannonia they were allied to the Romans and assisted in some operations in Italy. Paul relates the myth that Narses, the Emperor's representative in Italy in revenge for his recall to Constantinople,

> *"soon sent messengers to the nation of the Langobards, urging them to abandon the barren fields of Pannonia and come and take possession of Italy, teeming with every sort of riches."* [161]

Having described their arrival in Italy, Paul proceeds to give extensive and detailed description of the origin, and history of the provinces of Italy then extant.

Book III

In this Book two stories are related which have strong echoes with Ireland and its heritage of Round Towers. The first concerns an incursion by the Langobards into Gaul. Near Nice a holy man, Hospitius, warned the local people of the invaders imminent arrival and while they and his fellow monks fled, he himself repaired to a tower. When the Langobards approached:

"He showed himself to them through a window in a tower. But when they, going around the tower, sought an entrance through which they could pass in to him, and found none at all, two of them climbed upon the roof and uncovered it." [162]

The second story illustrates the importance of symbols to ancient peoples and has parallels to stories concerning the treatment of Irish chieftains by Prince John on his arrival in Ireland.

> *"And six thousand of the Saxons who survived the war made a vow that they would cut neither beard nor hair until they avenged themselves upon their Suabian enemies."* [163]

---

[159] *Pannonia was a province of the Roman Empire bounded north and east by the Danube and is now a part of Hungary.*

[160] *An ancient city now Sremska Mitrovica in modern Serbia.*

[161] *Book II, Chapter V.*

[162] *Book III, Chapter II.*

[163] *Book III, Chapter VII.*

The status of the Roman population in the areas ruled by the Langobards was very much that of 2nd class citizens with severe penalties placed on Langobards of either sex who intermarried. This is one of the most important passages in Paul's history, as it furnishes almost the only existing statement of the condition of the Roman population under the early Langobard kings. [164]

Book IV

By 600 A.D. the position of the Emperor in Italy had weakened considerably and the settlement of the Langobards had effectively become permanent. This led to direct negotiations with the Langobards:

> "Also at this time king Agilulf sent his secretary Stablicianus to Constantinople to the Emperor Focas" [165]

It was at this time that Paul's own ancestors were taken as slaves by the Avars, but finally his great-grandfather, Lopichis escaped and returned to Italy. In a chapter dealing with death of king Agilulf we find the following reference:

> "About these times the holy Columban…after he had built a monastery in Gaul in the place called Luxovium (Luxeuil), came into Italy, and was kindly received by the king of the Langobards, and built a convent in the Cottian Alps which is called Bobium (Bobbio) and is forty miles distant from the city of Ticinum." [166]

St. Columban had been born about 543 and died 615, the same year as Agilulf. He was a major figure in the conversion of the Langobards.

Book V

In this book we discover that the Emperor Constans visited Rome in 663 A.D., the first emperor to do so for nearly two centuries:

> "He left Naples and proceeded to Rome. At the sixth mile-stone from the city, pope Vitalian came to meet him with his priests and the Roman people." [167]

---

[164] *Book III, Chapter xvi.*

[165] *Book IV, Chapter xxxiv.*

[166] *Book IV, Chapter XLI.*

[167] *Book V, Chapter XI.*

Book VI

The importance of astronomy and astrology permeates the work and eclipses and shooting stars are frequently seen as harbingers of disaster:

> "In these times during the eight indiction (A.D. 680) the moon suffered and eclipse; also an eclipse of the sun occurred at almost the same time on the fifth day before the Nones of May about the tenth hour of the day. And presently there followed a very severe pestilence for three months..." [168]

And again:

"Afterwards in the month of February at noonday there arose a star in the west which set with a great flash in the direction of the east. Then in the month of March there was an eruption of Bebius (Vesuvius)..." [169]

Writing of dissension amongst Langobards Paul gives examples of its consequences and directly attributes functionality to his history:

> "We put these things into this history especially for this purpose, that nothing further of a like character may happen through the evil of dissension." [170]

King Liutprand reigned from 712 to 744 A.D. and brought the Langobards to the summit of their power. He largely discontinued trial by combat incorporated much Roman law and "he encouraged the movement in favour of the autonomy of Italy against Byzantium." [171] It is at this juncture that Paul's history ends and it was only 50 years later that the Langobards were overthrown and largely incorporated into the growing Frankish Empire as is stated in notes:

> "Hadrian who then occupied the papal throne, urgently besought Charlemagne for immediate aid. Charlemagne traversed the passes of the Alps, marched against Desiderius, and laid siege to Pavia. In June, 774, the city was taken, Desiderius was led into captivity and the kingdom of the Langobards was destroyed." [172]

In his introduction Macalister, dealing with this section adds an important note:

> "It is worth passing notice that on folio 116 lines 9 ff., there is a brief account of the translation of the relics of St Peter's daughter Petronilla, and a copy of the inscription alleged to have been set over them. This is possibly the missing 'Story of Petronilla,' which O'Curry reports as having once been included in the Codex, but of which no trace now remains." [173]

---

[168] *Book VI, Chapter V.*

[169] *Book VI, Chapter IX.*

[170] *Book VI, Chapter XXIV.*

[171] *Book VI, Chapter LVIII.*

[172] *Book VI, Chapter LVIII.*

[173] *The Book of Lismore. Introduction by R.A.S. Macalister Manuscripts Commission 1950 pg. xxi.*

Section IX

Marco Polo travels

While some writers have suggested that both the person and travels of Marco Polo are fictitious, the conventional wisdom suggests that Polo was born of a trading Venetian family in 1254 and that he died in 1324. What is not in doubt is that the *"publication"* of the travels in 1298 caused a sensation and within the lifetime of the author over 80 versions were in circulation. Later the notoriety of the piece continued at a reduced level but by the dawning of the *"Age of Discovery"* its vogue was restored and it became one of the first manuscripts to be printed. It is known that Columbus had a copy and the western love of the produce of the east, in particular silks and spices, did not preclude an interest in what appeared then and was in fact, a far more sophisticated civilization than that which then pertained in Europe. The text is descriptive rather than literary and the primary motivation would appear to be to encourage trade, suggest trade routes, outline cultural habits and generally assist those travelling to the East.

The version produced in the Book of Lismore is true to the original but *"this translation, of which there is no other copy known begins abruptly."* [174] It represents, perhaps 30% of the original manuscript and is largely unabridged. The source is uncertain but one suggestion is that it follows a translation made by Pipini which was taken *"from Tartar to Latin."* There are two well-known translations from the Irish, the first by Colonel Henry Yule [175] and the other by Whitley Stokes. [176]

In outlining some of the interesting content I have chosen to select material both from the Lismore text and that of the recognized full text. There is an undoubted admiration for the Tartar or Mongol Empire that is seen to parallel that of Rome. The use of *"paper money"* by the Mongols is eons ahead of its time and the focus on the *"Arabian horse"* is notable. Communication via a horse courier system over hundreds if not thousands of miles predates that of Wells Fargo by some seven centuries. The use of trees to define road perimeters, and the descriptions of the use of coal as a source of fuel are novel.

---

[174] *Introduction pg. xxi.*

[175] *National Manuscripts of Ireland: Account of facsimiles of National Manuscripts of Ireland from the earliest extant specimens to A.D. 1719. edited by John Thomas Gilbert. Ireland: Alex. Thom & Co. (Ltd), 1884. pg. 125.*

[176] *The Gaelic abridgement of the Book of Ser. Marco Polo. By Whitley Stokes. Zeitschrift für celtische philology herausgegeren von Kuno Meyer und L. Chr. Stern. pgs 245-273 and 362-438.*

Little sensitivity to European or ecclesiastical predilections is displayed when in Tibet Polo comments that tokens are held by women for each man who sleeps with them before marriage – *"And she who has most tokens and can show that she has had most lovers and that most men have lain with her is the most highly esteemed and the most acceptable as a wife; for they say that she is the most favoured of the gods…Obviously the country is a fine one to visit for a lad from sixteen to twenty-four"* [177] and further when he explains that Yogis as part of their probation final test are required to bring in attractive maidens when *"they touch them on various parts of the body and embrace and fondle them and instill into them the uttermost of earthly bliss. If the man thus caressed lies completely motionless without any reaction to the maiden's touch, he passes muster and is admitted to their order. If on the other hand his member reacts to the touch, they will not keep him, but expel him forthwith…"* [178] There is a fascinating description of a whaling expedition which is evocative and similar to descriptions in Moby Dick [179] and we must also remember that this was the age of the crusades [180] as in the appellation of *"Saracen dogs."*

One of the more colourful stories concerns Russia where a description is given of a wife who relieves herself on the way home from a night's drinking and *"the cold was so fierce that the hairs of her thighs froze on to the grass, so that she could not move and cried aloud. Her husband reeling drunk and distressed at her plight, stooped down and began to breathe over her, hoping to melt the ice by the warmth of his breath. But while he breathed, the moisture of his breath congealed and so the hairs of his beard froze together with his wife's and he too was stuck there unable to move for pain. Before they could budge from the spot, other helpers had to come and break the ice."* [181]

A description in Book I Section 34 [182] when the attempted removal of a flagstone in the Church of St. John the Baptist in Samarkand at the instigation of the Moslem community can be directly related to a similar story in the Wars of Charlemagne concerning the Church of St James. [183] An account of military strategy in dealing with frightened horses [184] is equally paralleled in Charlemagne suggesting that Polo's transcriber, Rustichello of Pisa was *"enhancing"* his story from known and recognized existing tales. Finally, a description of an attempted invasion of Japan [185] by the Tartars should be particularly noted as this event is undoubtedly historically accurate.

---

[177] *Do. pgs. 172-173.*

[178] *Do. pg. 281.*

[179] *Do. pg. 297.*

[180] *Do. pgs. 306-7.*

[181] *Do. pg. 334.*

[182] *Do. pgs. 255-257.*

[183] *In an interesting parallel at Castle Ellis, the old church was dedicated to St. John and about the year 1570, John Devereux, the Protestant Bishop of the diocese went to take down the statue of St. John. It fell on him and killed him.*

[184] *Do. pg. 391.*

[185] *Book III, section 46-153 pgs. 405-409.*

Section X

This section includes:

The Settling of the Manor (or Household) of Tara

Ostensibly this middle-Irish tract treats of the political structures of Ireland but is in fact used as a vehicle to describe the mythological origins of Irish civilization and the *"five Invasions"* of the country. The text occurs in the Yellow Book of Lecan and the Book of Lismore with the former providing the more complete version. It is notable for *"curious folklore, its vocabulary, and its placenames."* The story is interspersed with poems ascribed to the key narrator Fintan.

The starting point for the story is the settling of a dispute by reference to heritage and history. During the reign of Diarmait Mac Cerbaill (whose life and death are further explored in the following sections) the power of the kingship of Tara becomes a matter of dispute. [186] The Uí Neill in conference in Magh Bregh considered that *"the demesne of Tara seemed excessive to them"* and decided that the nobility of Ireland *"would not partake of the feast of Tara until the settling of the manor of Tara was determined."* [187] Following consideration of the appropriate authority to make a judgement it is agreed that the arbitration should fall to Fintan son of Bóchra *"son of Bith, son of Noah"* who was born before, and lived in Tul Tuinde at the time of the Deluge but now resided in Munster.

Fintan comes with eighteen companies *"nine before him and nine behind"* and remained with them *"forty days and nights"* until the assembly was complete. On his arrival Fintan responds to the hospitality he receives:

> *"I am sure of your welcome as every son is sure of his fostermother, and this is my fostermother...the island in which ye are, even Ireland, and the familiar knee of this island is the hill on which ye are, namely Tara."* [188]

---

[186] *The settling of the manor of Tara. Trans and edited by R.I. Best. Ériu: The Journal of the school of Irish Learning. Vol. IV – Parts I & II 1908-1910 reprinted 1978 pgs. 121-172 121pg.*

[187] *Do. pg. 127.*

[188] *Do. pg. 129.*

Fintan proceeds directly to narrate tales of the early arrivals and invasions of Ireland in one lay we hear:

> *"Thereupon the hosts of Eber and Eremon*
> *departed eastwards,*
> *And after loss of their force they occupied*
> *Ireland, on escaping from Egypt."* [189]

And in more prosaic but specific terms:

> *"From the children of Míl of Spain and from the Greeks are we sprung. After the building of the Tower of Nimrod, and the confusion of tongues, we came into Egypt, upon the invitation of Pharaoh King of Egypt. Nél son of Fénius and Goedel Glas were our chiefs while we were in the south. Hence we are called Féne from Fénius, that is the Féne, and Gaels from Gaedel Glas"* [190]

The flight of the Israelites from Egypt precipitates the departure and final arrival via Spain in Ireland, *"because our forefathers went not with the Egyptians in pursuit of the people of God, they dreaded Pharaoh's wrath against them should he return"* [191]

Fintan in his description of the partitions of Ireland provides an interesting observation that there is *"knowledge in the west, battle in the north, prosperity in the east, music in the south, kingship in the centre"*. [192] In an aside we are told that Fintan had been given berries in ancient times and from these sprang the ancient trees of Tortu and Mugna, the latter is also featured in *"Fingen's Nightwatch."* Fintan then delivers his judgement on the dispute confirming the extant divisions and powers in Ireland, *"let it be as we have found it…we shall not go contrary to the arrangement which Trefuilngid Tre-eochair has left us, for he was an angel of God, or he was God himself."* [193]

In a final lay Fintan returns to the invasions of Ireland:

> *"Five invasions, best of deeds,*
> *The land of Ireland has undergone.*
> *I have been here a while after them*
> *Until the days of the sons of Míl."* [194]

---

[189] *Do. pg. 139.*

[190] *Do. pg. 141.*

[191] *Do. pg. 143.*

[192] *Do. pg. 147.*

[193] *Do. pg. 155.*

[194] *Do. pg. 161.*

The Colloquy of Cennfáelad and Fintan

This piece includes just ten lines. A more complete version of this colloquy is provided in Laud [195] 610, fo. 57b and is there titled *"Interrogatio Cinnfáelad."* The piece is in fact an extract from The Settling of the Manor of Tara. The following extract taken from the Laud manuscript dealing with 'features of Ireland' adequately presents the sense of the piece:

> *"Her learning, her foundation, her teaching, her alliance, her judgment, her chronicles, her counsels, her stories, her histories, her science, her comeliness, her eloquence, her beauty, her modesty (lit. blushing), her bounty, her abundance, her wealth – from the western part in the west."*

Cennfáelad was a major scholar and poet who died circa 679. He was a member of the Cenél nÉogain and is credited with major developments in the structure of Irish poetry. He was *"the first poet quoted in the Irish Annals, being referred to as sapiens, a technical term denoting a head teacher."* Many important texts have been attributed to him.

The opening portion of Agallamh Becc

[The little colloquy which is repeated in a later section.]

As this is repeated in detail in the final section it is inappropriate to comment on it here. Why it should have been repeated in the Book is unknown.

A Story of Aedh Baclámh

This is a constituent construct in the cycle of tales concerning King Dermot Mac Cearbhaill. It nominally concerns the King's spear-carrier or envoy, Aedh Baclámh, who following a year of illness is dispatched by the King on a circuit of Ireland to confirm the peaceful status of the country and to validate the loyalty of the king's subjects. Aedh on his arrival in Connaught had visited the house of Aedh Guaire of Kinelfechin in Hy-Many. Agiolandus sought a reception in accord with his status and so irritated Aedh Guaire that the latter murdered him.

King Dermot then sought revenge and justice for his envoy and Aedh Guaire,

> *"…fled to bishop Senan, for it was the one mother they had. Senan the bishop again goes with him to Ruadhan of Lorrha, for it was two sisters to Ruadhan that had nursed bishop Senan: Cael and Ruadhnait were their names."* [196]

---

[195] *Archbishop William Laud, 1573-1645 was a noted classical scholar. He was executed and his papers were deposited at the Bodleian Library in Oxford.*

[196] *O'Grady, Standish (trans.) "A story of Aedh Baclamh" Silva Gaedelica Vol.II [1892] pgs. 70-75 pg. 71.*

The King eventually captured Aedh Guaire and despite the endeavours of Ruadhan he refused to concede the freedom of his captor. St. Brendan son of Finnlogh then arrived to plead the case and Dermot set the saint a task which he believed could not be achieved:

> "…were ye to give me fifty horses, blue-eyed and with golden bridles, I would yield you up Aedh Guaire." [197]

However Brendan not only passed this and provided other miraculous manifestations of his power that Dermot acknowledged his defeat:

> "'Alas,' he said 'for the iniquitous contest that ye have waged against me: seeing it is Ireland's good that I pursue and to preserve her discipline and royal right; but 'tis Ireland's unpeace and murderousness that ye endeavour after.'" [198]

So frustrated was Dermot that he and Ruadhan swapped a series of curses but eventually Dermot released Aedh Guaire to Ruadhan and upon the king *"came great repentance for having pitted his wrath against the clergy…"*

The tale is followed by a significant lay spoken by the King which appears somewhat incongruous and has little direct relation to the story. It directly relates back to the destruction by Dermot of the famous *"ridgebeam"* of his mansion at Tara which the King had thrown into the sea to avoid a prophetic inference of its part in his future death. The lay also contains other allusions to the king's death.

The primary object of this tale appears to be to confirm the primacy of church authority over any secular authority even where the power so wielded is utilised to protect a criminal. This theme reverberates in other early Irish stories including some within the Book of Lismore.

The Prophecy of Bec Mac Dé

Consists of 20 *"staccato ejaculations on the evils of the world."* *"This is essentially part of the 'Diarmait' cycle with which section X is occupied, as it was repeated to Diarmait in the course of the events described in Aided Diarmata."* [199]

Bec mac Dé was the most renowned seer of his era and his death in 553 A.D. is recorded in the Annals. His prophecy is central to the story of Diarmait as it was he who provided the detailed description of the nature of the king's death.

---

[197] *Do. pg. 72.*

[198] *Do. pg. 73.*

[199] *The Book of Lismore. Introduction by R.A.S. Macalister Manuscripts Commission 1950 pg. xxii.*

Story of Becan and the Nun's Cow

This short enigmatic and poetic tract explores the rights and privileges of civil and ecclesiastical authorities. The piece relates that Bresal son of King Diarmait in preparation for a feast to honour his father seeks unsuccessfully to purchase a nun's prize cow. He then steals and butcher's the cow but as the feast begins the nuns arrives and screams out and the King responds:

"'Unjust is what thou hast done, saith the king' (to his son), 'to outrage the nun as regards her cow while she was in her church, and to resist my kingship and my discipline. For it is not an ancestral usage for thee to do so. And thou shalt be killed by me for the deed thou hast done.'" [200]

Having executed his promise the King is overcome by grief and seeks the intercession of Colum Cille to redeem his action. The Saint directs him to Becan of Ulaidh who on their arrival at his Church proclaims:

"'Under the earth thou parricide!' So Diarmait went into the earth as far as his knees. 'The protection is without stay, O Becan' says Colum Cille: 'for the king hath come to thee to ask thee to forgive him and to restore his son to life." Becan raised his right hand and thrice made prayer to resuscitate Bresal son of Diarmait, and at each prayer he brought fifty Bresals out of hell; and at the last prayer Bresal son of Diarmait came with the last batch of them.'" [201]

What is central to this piece is the Colum Cille who holds a higher status in the family of Saints requires intersession from Becan. This suggests a distinction of patronage rather than of status a difference which is well developed in modern church usage where we are well acquainted with prayers to *"patron saints"* associated with particular facets of human experience.

The Battle of Cúl Dreimne

The Battle of Cúl Dreimne is a companion piece and can be considered as a prelude to the Death of Diarmait Mac Cerbaíll. While it is certain that the battle took place near Ben Bulben in Sligo in 560 or 561 A.D. the cause and protagonists are shrouded in mystery and

"the story of battle of Cúl Dreimne became highly fictionalized, indeed mythologized" [202]

The core of the cause as set out in the later narrations involves a dispute between Diarmait Mac Cerbaíll and Colum Cille. In the Annals of Tigernach for 559 the record of the killing of Curnán by Diarmait while under the protection of Colum Cille is the source.

---

[200] *Stokes, Whitley. Anecdota Oxoniensia Lives of the Saints from the Book of Lismore. Edited with a translation, notes and indices by Whitley Stokes. Oxford: Clarendon Press, 1890. pgs. xvii-xviii.*

[201] *Do pg. xxviii.*

[202] *Lacey, Brian. The battle of Cúl Dreimne – a reassessment. Ireland: RSAI, Volume 133, 2003 pgs. 78-85.*

In another account the copying of a manuscript by Colum Cille and the famous subsequent judgement by Diarmait in favour of Finnian of Moville *"le gach boin a boinin…le gach leabhur a labhrán"* is the prelude to this Battle of the Books.

However, as set out by Brian Lacey *"neither of the stated reasons for the battle can be said to be compellingly believable."*[203] What appears much more likely is that the cause was the attempt by the Cenél Cairpre to expand their power further north of the Duff into what is now south-Donegal.

In the Annals of Ulster we are given a brief summary of the event:

> *"The battle of Cúil Dreimne, in which 3000 fell, [won] over Diarmait mac Cerbaíll…They prevailed through the prayers of Colum Cille."* [204]

The intersession by Colum's prayers is also recounted in the Annals of Tigernach. We are told that feelings of guilt subsequently led to Colum's departure for Scotland, an account which is related by Lydon in the Making of Ireland:

> *"The penitent saint was later told by his anam chara ('soul friend', the typical confessor of the Irish church) that he must go into exile as a penance."* [205]

But this rationale for Colum's departure is highly unlikely as according to Lacey quoting Adomnán in Vita Columbae there was a considerable interval prior to the departure:

> *"In the second year after the battle of Cul-drebene, the forty-second year of his age Columba sailed away from Ireland to Britain to be a pilgrim for Christ."* [206]

The Death of Diarmait Mac Cerbaíll

Diarmait mac Cerbaíll was High King of Ireland until his death in 565. He has gained notoriety from his entries in the various sagas and annals. He was the last king to follow the pagan rituals of inauguration on his coronation in circa 558 or 560 A.D. These rituals have been described by Lydon:

> *"The sacred nature of his kingship was symbolized at his inauguration by his solemn marriage to the goddess of his land, a custom which was so important that it survived the influence of Christianity until much later in the middle ages. For the new religion to gain even a foothold it would first of all have to overcome this pagan prop of kingship and gain the king himself."* [207]

---

[203] *Do. pg. 78.*

[204] *Do. pg. 80.*

[205] *Lydon, James. The making of Ireland: from ancient times to the present. U.K. Routledge, 1998. ix,425p pg. 9.*

[206] *Lacey, Brian. The battle of Cúl Dreimne – a reassessment. RSAI etc. pg. 81.*

[207] *Lydon, James. The making of Ireland: from ancient times to the present. U.K. Routledge, 1998. ix,425p pg. 5.*

He was killed in 565 at Ráith Bec in Mag Line in Ulster by Áed Dub mac Suibhne and following his death the power of the kingship of Tara went into decline for some time. The supernatural features prominently in accounts of his reign as is exemplified by an account 'druidic fences' created for the protection of his forces at the Battle of Cúl Dreimne.

However, it is the accounts of his death that are the most important in the sagas. He sought Druidic predictions and tried to avoid these as in the case of a beam in Tara which he had thrown in the sea following a prediction that it would play a part in his death. He was subsequently told that he would die *"by slaughter, drowning and burning."* The roof beam of Tara was recovered by Banbán and used in his hall, *"the shirt and mantle and ale and bacon are duly produced for Diarmait. Diarmait goes to leave Banbán's hall, but Áed Dub, waiting at the door strikes him down and sets fire to the hall. Diarmait crawls into an ale vat to escape the flames and is duly killed by the falling beam."* Thus all the prophecies concerning his death are fiulfilled.

This tract illustrates to an extraordinary degree the connectivity, sophistication, transmission, synergy and transmutation of mythology across the entire Indo-European civilisations over a relatively short period. In an interesting book [208] on the transfer of educational concepts across cultures Masahiro Tanaka develops the thesis that the educational systems of one nation cannot be transferred to another without profound adaptations and modifications. This theses is an enhancement of the ideas of Schriewer who proposed that the very models chosen *"are selected based on the prevailing interests of the import nation and then adapted to their specific situations and needs."* [209] This theorem could equally be applied to the transmission of mythologies across distinct cultures.

Duties of an Ideal King

This is a significant didactic poem that is available in several early versions the most complete of which is that contained in the Book of Leinster. [210] The version in the Book of Lismore has been credited to Dubh dá Thuath who lived circa 8th Century. The poem may have some connections with the kingdom of Cashel and according to O'Donoghue:

> *"one may judge that the poem was originally shorter than it stands at present. Poetry of a didactic nature such as this lends itself to additions and interpolations."* [211]

---

[208] *Tanaka, Masahiro. The cross-cultural transfer of educational concepts and practices: a comparative study. U.S. Symposium Books, 2005. 152p.*

[209] *Schriewer, J. Discourse formation in Comparative Education. Germany: Peter Lang.*

[210] *Advice to a Prince. Tadhg O'Donoghue. Ériu: The Journal of the School of Irish Learning, Dublin. Vol. IX [1921-23] reprinted 1974 pgs. 43-54.*

[211] *Do. pg. 44.*

There are thirty seven stanzas in the translation provide by O'Donoghue. In verse eight we are informed:

> *"The things that are best for a prince during his reign are truth,*
> *Mercy and silence; those that are worst for a king's honour*
> *Are straying from the truth and adding to the false."*

And in stanza seventeen:

> *"There are four things a prince should have, in order that he*
> *May do well both here and hereafter; peace among his*
> *Tribes, protection of churches, reproof of treason, help for*
> *the weak."*

We are later told that *"love hides blemishes and evil"* and in verse twenty four that reason is superior to physical power; *"The head is nobler than the members."* As in many of the other tracts in the Book of Lismore, we are left in little doubt about the importance and imperative of social order as in verses twenty-six to thirty-three we are told that sons should follow their father's calling:

> *"-'tis his due to follow in the calling of his family."* [verse 28]

Cert Gach Rígh Co Réil

This is a poem of 45 quatrains or in some versions 59 quatrains. It outlines the privileges and duties of the kings of Clann Néill. The version in the Book of Leinster is *"besides being the oldest version…the only version which gives the name of the author."* [212] It is a parallel piece to the earlier piece Settling of the household of Tara and the Prohibitions and Privileges of the Kings of Ireland which follows in Section XI. One version of the poem contains an address to King *"Aedh Oirdnidhe asking him to exempt the clergy from military service"* [213] thus allowing the piece to be dated to circa A.D. 815 when Aedh was King.

---

[212] O'Donoghue, Tadhg [trans.] Cert cech righ go réil. [In] Miscellany presented to Kuno Meyer. 1912 pgs 258-277. pg. 258.

[213] Do. pg. 259.

Unlike Settling and Prohibitions this piece has as its primary focus appropriate methods for the creation and maintenance of power by ruthless means where necessary:

> *"Take hostages from all, so that you may be a keen prince,*
> *And be able to chastise, on every business about which you go."* [5] [214]

> *Put harsh gyves on a prisoner from afar,*
> *For his death is preferable to his escaping without leave."* [8] [215]

> *"Let every wanton rebel be put to death at once;"* [45] [216]

> *"If any man has committed theft, it is not honourable for you*
> *If he get shelter in palace or sanctuary."* [61] [217]

This final quatrain is particularly interesting in the light of the approach advocated in Aed Baclámh. However justice and consideration should be central to the application of power:

> *"Do not take sides with the strong; but truly serve,*
> *So that both yourself and your descendants may rule brilliantly."* [65] [218]

> *"honour every man as if he were a king or prince."* [31] [219]

The privileges due are outlined but are not of particular note:

> *"An hundred dinners are also due from each full stead*
> *For the upkeep of the host that comes from the north with Aed."* [58] [220]

A sub-theme in the piece concerns the protection of and support to be provided to the clergy and the church:

> *"Leave the churches untaxed during your course of clear success."* [14]

---

[214] *Do. pg. 261.*

[215] *Do. pg. 261.*

[216] *Do. pg. 271.*

[217] *Do. pg. 275.*

[218] *Do. pg. 275.*

[219] *Do. pg. 267.*

[220] *Do. pg. 273.*

There is a significant misogynous element within this poem which is not apparent in any other sections of the book and occurs in several quatrains:

> *"Esteem the clergy; keep control over their dwelling; protect them against women, good noble son of Niall"* [20] [221]

> *"There are seven royal maidens that ruin tribes,*
> *And sleep with every silly fellow though an active warrior*
> *be unwilling"* [42] [222]

> *"Should a woman commit adultery among the laity or the clergy,*
> *Let nobody be put to death for it, except the guilty one."* [51] [223]

This is undoubtedly a poem rich in texture and theme that will reward further significant study and exploration.

Airne Fíngein - Fingen's Night Watch

This tale originates in the 9th or 10th Century and is part of the Cycles of the Kings. Fingein, the central figure in the tale, has visits each Samhain Eve by an *"otherworld woman"* called Rothníam who on each visit narrates to him fifty prophecies. Only twelve are given in the text and amongst these are:

> [3] A tree that has been hidden in Ireland since before the Flood is discovered. This tree is an offspring of the tree of Eden and will provide an eternal benefit. It is called Mugna.

> [6] The five principal roads of Ireland are revealed, The Slige Midluchra, Slige Cúaland, the Slige Asail, the Slige Tola and the Slige Mór. [224]

> [10] Concerns the erection of the palisade upon Rath Aildinne *"whatever the builders and smiths used to lift of it in one day, that fell down in the morning."* It also relates that the three rivers, The Suir, the Nore and the Barrow merge and flow into one estuary.

---

[221] *Do. pg. 265.*

[222] *Do. pg. 271.*

[223] *Do. pg. 273.*

[224] *Vendryes, Joseph. (ed) Airne Fíngein. Dublin: Dublin Institute for Advanced Studies, 1953. xxiii, 95p.*

[225] *Do.*

[15] This section is particularly important as it appears only in the version of the tale of Airne Fíngein given in the Book of Lismore. Conn who holds the kingship of Ireland for fifty-three years is the best king in Ireland before the coming of Christianity. There is no disease, no bad weather, or theft in his reign and the land is fertile. *"In fact Ireland becomes a Land of Promise (Tír Tairngire) under his sway."* [225]

In an interesting and valuable study of this tract [226] Tom Peete Cross has raised issues of comparative storiology. His central query concerns the literary origins of the tale and whether it *"is an independent Irish invention comparable to those framing devices which have enjoyed great vogue in those literatures of Western Europe"* or is *"a sign of the influence on Irish of other literatures."* He does not, however, raise the possibility of transmission or synergetic development in the other direction.

---

[226] *Fingen's Night-Watch: Airne Fingein. Cross, Tome Peete & Brown, Arthur. The Romantic Review. U.S. 1918 pgs. 29-47.*

The Book of Rights sets out the privileges and stipends of the Irish Kings and sub-kings and is available in several versions in various old Irish manuscripts. It represents a blending of civil and ecclesiastical authority in a sophisticated and minute list of dependencies. It represents an attempt by the early church in Ireland to end the endemic and petty conflicts within the country. There are two classic translations, the first by John O'Donovan [227] and the second by Myles Dillon. [228] The work is ascribed to Saint Benen or Benignus who was a disciple of Saint Patrick.

> "Here begins the Book of Rights. It tells of the rents and stipends of Ireland which Benén son
> of Sescnén, Patrick's cantor, ordained, as related in the Book of Glendalough" [229]

In the case of rights the following example is representative:

> "Two thousand choice boars to the hill…
> A thousand cows in flocks
> Of wealth from the Déisi,
> Though he say it(?).
>
> This is a tribute on behalf of the territory at first,
> A sage in reckoning has preserved it…
> Not because of the lowly rank of those for whom it has been settled,
> But because of the noble rank of the plain of Cashel" [230]

A listing of internal tributes from within the Kingdom of Munster is also provided in minute detail:

> "A thousand oxen from the Déisi
> A thousand good sheep,
> A thousand white-fringed cloaks,
> A thousand cows after calving" [231]

---

[227] O'Donovan, John. Leabhar na g-Ceart or the Book of Rights. U.S.: Adamant Media Corporation, 2000. 406p.

[228] Lebor na Cert: The book of Rights. Edited by Myles Dillon. Dublin: Published for the Irish Texts Society by the Educational Co. of Ireland, 1962 xxv,194p [the quotations are taken from the online version of the text at www.maryjones.us/ctexts/cert. and follow its pagination.]

[229] Do. pg. 1.

[230] Do. pg. 6.

[231] Do. pg. 10.

The stipends given by the king of Cashel to the kings within his realm are similarly detailed:

> *"eight slaves, eight swarthy women*
> *And ten ships to the king of the Déisi*
> *Eight shields, eight swords for smiting*
> *And eight horses from over the sea."* [232]

And again:

> *"The stipend of the king of the Déisi*
> *From the king of Cashel, examine it,*
> *Is a gold-hilted sword, a famous horse,*
> *And a ship fully rigged."* [233]

The importance and central role of the Bard or historian is not forgotten and in this regard the narrator is not above ensuring that his listeners and employer can have no doubts:

> *"Tara does not belong to him*
> *Unless there be a reliable historian*
> *Who may tell his lord*
> *The stipend of each man."* [234]

As with many of the early manuscripts the magical quality and significance of numbers is apparent as they are regularly repeated and juxtaposed:

> *"The noble king of the Déisi is entitled*
> *To eight good horses that will be prized,*
> *Eight green cloaks, and*
> *Eight brooches of findruine."* [235]

It is particularly noteworthy that the magical number nine which is of huge importance in early Celtic tradition is nowhere used in a text of almost unending numeric listings.

---

[232] *Do. pg. 12.*

[233] *Do. pg. 14.*

[234] *Do. pg. 47.*

[235] *Do. pg. 52.*

A Chaisil as Dimbrig Soin

This is an elegy in 34 quatrains for King Feidlimid Mac Crimthainn. He was king of Munster from 820 to 846 A.D. and was a member of the Eóganacht Clann. He was a noted Cleric, Abbot and according to Craig Haggart *one of the most enigmatic figures in early medieval Irish history.* [236] F. J. Byrne has provided a concise summation of his life and career:

"At a most critical era in Irish history, when devastating Viking raids were succeeded by permanent base-camps and settlements, Feidlimid never once devoted his arms to attacking these heathen foreigners but distinguished his martial career by burning and plundering some of the greatest of Irish monasteries – Kildare, Gallen, Durrow, Clonfert and above all, Clonmacnoise – captured and maltreated the abbot of Armagh, allowed the abbot of Cork to die without the comforts of religion in his prison at Cashel, and was finally struck down by the vengeance of St. Ciarán." [237]

He would appear to have been installed in 838 A.D. as high king but in 841 was defeated by Niall Caille and,

> *"The crozier of the devout Feidlimid*
> *Was abandoned in the blackthorns*
> *Niall, mighty in combat, took it*
> *By right of victory in battle with swords."* [238]

The presence of this poem on such a significant figure in Munster history is hardly surprising but his membership of the Eóganacht Clann made it virtually inevitable. The poem in the Book of Lismore begins:

> *"O Cashel, this is weakness*
> *Without Feidlimid son of Crimthan!*
> *O territory of Tuathal! Sad the deed!*
> *Without thy herdsman protecting thee."* [239]

[236] Haggart, Craig. Feidlimid mac Crimthainn and the óentu Maile Ruain [online article].

[237] Byrne, FJ. Irish kings and high-kings. U.K.: 1973.

[238] Annals of Ulster.

[239] Lives of Saints from the Book of Lismore translated by Whitley Stokes Oxford: Clarendon Press, 1890 pg. xxxi.

Trí Gaire in Domain (The Three Cries of the World)

This piece contains short notes, including the three cries of the world, for which Whitley Stokes has provided a brief résumé:

"the cry of the Israelites when they entered the Red Sea, the cry of Hell when Christ carried off his prey from it, the cry of Doomsday when the righteous separate from the sinners.)." [240]

Re Cethra Neithit Samailter Gloir int Saegail

This is a further short note also summarised by Stokes:

"on the four things that resemble earthly glory (wind, smoke, sleep and a flower): on the worst sin (pride); and the greatest good (humility)." [241]

Nonbar Noebh sil Conuire

This is a short list *"in prose and verse"* of the nine saints from the race of Conaire. One of these saints was Saint Ciara who was a daughter of Duibhre a member of the illustrious family of Muskerry. Initially she was based in Ely O'Carroll and then in Tech-telle in Westmeath before returning to Kilcrea near Cork where she established a monastery. In his narration of her Baring-Gould [242] provides a short poetic extract,

"Nine persons of the race of Conaire
By learned persons called
Three lights, three seniors, three virgins
Commemorated by the ancient sages

These are the three caileachs (nuns)
Who freely gave their love to Christ
Ciara-Scach, Gobinait, with devotion
And Sciach, daughter of Meachner."

Saint Bearchán or Ferdaleithe, who was a noted seer and is best known as the apocryphal author of the 'Prophecy of Bearchán,' was a descendant as was Saint Moircheallog.

---

[240] Stokes, Whitley. *Lives of Saints from the Book of Lismore* Oxford: Clarendon Press, 1890 pgs. xxxi-xxxii.

[241] Do. pgs. xxxi-xxxii.

[242] Baring-Gould, S. *Lives of the Saints* U.K.: BiblioBazaar, 2009 416p pgs. 429-430.

The section contains the Victorious career of Cellachán of Cashel *"or the Wars between the Irishmen and the Norsemen in the middle of the 10th Century"* [243] as well as various other miscellanea including *"Conchobor and the Kingship of the Ulaid."* It is largely panegyric in style and substance. According to Bugge [244] and Ryan [245] the piece was written as a repost from the side of the McCarthys to the approach portrayed in the *Cogadh* [246] which favoured the perspective of the O'Briens. Ryan further challenges the views of O'Curry and O'Donovan who considered the text as merely *"semi-historical"* but according to Ryan it must be considered in the light that the *"purpose of the Caithréim is to extol 'the Eoganacht of Kerry, to which race Cellacháin belonged'"* [247]

Ryan suggests that that Irish linguistic style of the piece being *"bombastic striving after effects and the needless multiplication of adjectives"* [248] would date it to the end of the 11th or first quarter of the 12th century. He goes further and indicates that it was produced *"not later than 1118,"* the year in which Munster was divided [249] between the McCarthys and O'Briens because *"were the Caithréim composed between 1123 and 1138 or in the intervening period before the coming of the Normans, its attitude towards the Dál Chais would be, in my judgement, much more independent."* [250]

The text is written in epic style and contains as Ryan has suggested a large number of historic inaccuracies as well as total fabrications. It begins *"with a catalogue of the princes who ruled in Munster, and details of their sufferings under the Norsemen, and their contests until he emancipated them, subsequently to his election to the kingship of Munster."* [251]

---

[243] *Introduction the Book of Lismore pg. xxiii.*

[244] *Caithréim Cellacháin Caisil: The victorious career of Cellacháin of Cashel or The wars between the Irishmen and the Norsemen in the middle of the 10th Century. (the original Irish text edited with translation and notes) by Alexander Bugge Professor University of Christiania [Oslo]. Oslo: Det Norske Historiske Kilderkriftfond, 1905.*

[245] *"The historical content of the 'Caithréim Ceallagháin Chaisil' by The Rev. John Ryan. Journal RSAI, 1941 [Vol. LXXI] pgs 89-100.*

[246] *Cogadh Gaedhel re Gallaibh. The war of the Gaedhil with the Gaill, or, The invasions of Ireland by the Danes and other Norsemen. The original Irish Text, edited with translation and introduction. By James Henthorn Todd. London: Longmans, Green, Reader, and Dyer, 1867.*

[247] *Ryan. pg. 89.*

[248] *Ryan pg. 90.*

[249] *In the 12th century an actual partition of the province took place between the O'Brien kingdom of North Munster, Tuadmuma [Thomond], and the MacCarthy kingdom of South Munster, Desmuma [Desmond].*

[250] *Ryan pg. 91.*

[251] *National Manuscripts of Ireland. Gilbert pg. 125.*

The early battles with the Lochlannaigh [Scandinavians] are depicted in great detail and of particular interest is the campaign in Waterford. *"The next morning they made up their mind, namely to proceed to Port Lairge, the place where the women and families of the Lochlannachs were, and to burn the town. And they proceeded to the green of Port Lairge, but on the same day Sitric son of Turgeis arrived at Port Lairge with a division of six ships and a hundred on each ship of them. But they had not reached the land when the van of the host of Munster arrived at the city. The Danes closed the gates and began to defend the town. However, it was useless for them to engage in combat with the champions; for Cellacháin, and gentle Donnchadh, and Súilleabháin and Ribordan, and the quick, valiant soldiers of Munster leapt into the town. And the Danes were slaughtered in crowds by them, and the Norsemen were cut into pieces. Sitric left the town and went on board his ship, and his wife with him. And only one hundred fugitives of them reached their ships. The race of Eogan burned the town and plundered the district.*

And they proceeded thence to the country of the Deisi, and take hostages and pledges of Domnall son of Faelan. There was concluded a matrimonial alliance and made friendship with him and Gormflaith, the daughter of Buadachan, was given to him. Thence they proceeded into the territory of the Uí-Mic-Caille and the Uí Liathain and took hostages from them." [252]

In a further confrontation with the Danes Cellacháin is described as being outnumbered and attacked and *"Then Aed, the son of Domnall the descendant of Faelan, and Domnall the descendant of Niall of Magh Dachonn said 'We are twenty men of the Deisi, and let us remain behind the rest and avenge ourselves, before the body of the host overtakes us.' And they stopped and slew twenty heroes of the Norsemen, and only five of them came back to their people alive"* [253] However, these Deisi warriors are themselves subsequently killed [254] and Cellacháin is captured and after a major naval engagement near Dundalk which includes a group of *"Berserks"* [255] he is restored to his Kingship. This latter battle is according to Ryan a complete fantasy and indeed he informs us that Cellachán was captured not by the Danes but Irish Chieftains and was released rather than rescued. The King died in 952 A.D. He had *"established a limited suzerainty over the Norse of Munster and used them occasionally in his army. He was not particularly active in their destruction…"* [256] and *"In the wider political field, the Ireland of his day, he was an outstanding figure, occupying about third or fourth place in the ranking list of contemporary Kings".* [257]

---

[252] *Bugge pgs. 71-72.*

[253] *Bugge pg. 78.*

[254] *This campaign in the Deisi is significantly inaccurate as Cellacháin died march into the Deisi and killed over 2000 in a battle but was subsequently himself defeated by the Deisi and their then allies the men of Ossory.*

[255] *In Norse and Icelandic myth and folklore, a type of strong, fierce warrior, able to assume the form of certain animals, especially the bear and the wolf, and possessed at times by a wild frenzy which made him almost unconquerable in battle.*

[256] *Ryan pg. 99.*

[257] *Ryan pg. 100.*

Ní Téd a N-égen a N-aisgidh
Note on the above poem

These two sections are particularly important as they are the only pieces in the entire work essentially dealing with events relatively contemporaneous with the production of the Book of Lismore. They are also significant in dealing with aspects of the life of Fínghin the *"patron"* of the work. The poem is in 44 quatrains, *"written in long lines by a contemporary hand."* The poem has been ascribed to Mathghamhain (mac Domhnaill mheic Eoghain) Ó Dálaigh whom Standish O'Grady describes as *"hereditary rhymer to the Mac Carthys-Riach."* A detailed account of the poem and the following note (together with translations) has been produced by Brian Ó Cuív in the journal *Celtica*. [258]

The poem deals directly with the succession of Fínghin McCarthy Riabhach to his father, Diarmaid an Dúna Mac Carthaigh, Lord Cairbre's titles and estates following their 'violation' by *"a son of one of his brothers, Cormac mac Donnchaidh."* [259]   The Mac Carthaigh Riabhach clan was descended from the Eóganacht dynasty and Diarmaid succeeded to his lordship in 1452 holding it until 1468. In 1452 he married Ellen daughter of Teige O'Kennedy, Lord of Muskerry. Fínghin had regained his father's title by 1478 *"and continued to rule until his death in 1505 when he was succeeded by his brother Diarmaid."* Ó Cuív outlines the structure of the poem as follows:

> *"The first twenty-eight quatrains seem to be a comment on Fínghin Mac Carthaigh's position as ruler and central to this is the theme of the use of duress against his father by an unnamed kinsman who is identified in the accompanying note as Cormac mac Donnchaidh. Quatrains 29-36 are addressed directly to Fínghin and quatrains 37-40 continue on the lines of 1-28. The poem proper ends at quatrain 40 but there are four additional complimentary quatrains: 41-2 on Fínghin's wife Caitlín, 43 on Our Lady and 44 on St. Francis."* [260]

[258] Ó Cuív, Brian. *A poem for Finghin Mac Carthaigh Mac Carthaigh Riabhach*. Ireland: Celtica 15 (1983) pgs. 96-110.

[259] Ó Cuív, Brian. *A poem for Finghin Mac Carthaigh Mac Carthaigh Riabhach*. Ireland: Celtica 15 (1983) pg. 96.

[260] Ó Cuív, Brian. *A poem for Finghin Mac Carthaigh Mac Carthaigh Riabhach*. Ireland: Celtica 15 (1983) pg. 98.

The following short extracts from the poem are taken from Ó Cuív's translation:

"Duress does not go unrequited if what the learned men of [Ireland] say is true: [ ] the contract [ ] just; might never established a prescriptive right."

"Let all behold how the use of force against Fínghin's father turned out; it is a clear case of duress since he was deprived of the first turn (as ruler.)"

"He obtained proper restoration for his father [and] for himself too…"

"For three years – lasting torment – some of our kindred were in possession of our rights; we did not dare to speak of it since our pledged hostages happened to be incarcerated."

Echtra Taidhg Meic Céin: The Adventures of Tadg Son of Cian

This is a further tale of the otherworld but this time it is a fairy world or Tír na nÓg. It is profuse with biblical motifs and the apple tree is the central symbol, illustrating a merging of pagan and early Christian influences.

Taidhg, heir to a kingship in Munster, voyages across sea to recover his wife who has been kidnapped by Cathmann and his pirates. Following severe tempests he arrives at an unknown island. It is interesting to note that, unlike the scenario in most of the otherworld stories in the Book of Lismore the Otherworld is this time reached by sea voyage and that it is an Island rather than a subterranean region under a lake.

The Island is populated not only by beautiful women but also by many of the dead Celtic heroes and kings. There are two "dúns occupied and one vacant awaiting another hero – Taidhg". He is told of the nature of his future death and after a year in the otherworld which he and his force think is only a day during which they have neither eaten nor drunk [another recurring theme in these stories] they return home.

Cath Criona: The Battle of Crinna

This piece like the Siege of Knocklong relates to the career of King Cormac Mac Art. In their procession to the annual Feast of Tara at Samhain the men of Ulster led by King Fergus Blacktooth, Fergus Longhair and Fergus "Bregia" send emissaries ahead to check the status of their accommodation. They are advised that it is in a state of total dilapidation and disrepair. They are also informed that Tara is largely undefended and decide to avail of the opportunity for conquest, possibly using the insult to their dignity as just cause. Cormac unable to stand against this force seeks counsel and is advised to enlist the support of Teigue son of Clan a prince of Munster. Teigue is cajoled to support Cormac by an offer of land in the Kingdom of Tara.

Teigue's formation for the Battle of Crinna, with young men to the front, experienced men in the centre and *"grey-beards"* to the rear is at odds with contemporary Irish military practice. Having won the battle, Teigue is promised whatever land he can cross with his chariot in a given time. But Cormac ensures that it will not include Tara and indeed endeavours to cause the death of Teigue in treatment for wounds received during the battle. Teigue surmounts this treachery and eventually receives land in what is now modern Dublin and South-Meath.

Of particular note in interpreting this tract is that King Cormac Mac Art emerges with little credit, rather he appears as a conniving and ruthless schemer with little honour or respect for those who support his cause. The Cormac of Knocklong is portrayed in a more neutral hue.

Echtra Loegaire Meic Crimthainn: The Adventures of Loegaire Son of Crimthann

This tract from the Cycles of the Kings is another tale of the Otherworld or Mag Mell. What is particularly important is that the Otherworld is again located under a lake, in this case Énloch in County Roscommon. The story depicts the exploits of Loegaire and his forces who are recruited by Fiachna Mac Rétach of the Otherworld to recover his wife. Fiachna on receiving their support recites the March of the Faerie Host, the following is a verse from this important poem:

> *"They scatter the battalions of the foe,*
> *They ravage every land I have attacked,*
> *Splendidly they march to combat*
> *An impetuous, distinguished, avenging host."*

Loegaire and his forces succeed in recovering the errant wife after several battles. He marries Dér Gréine the daughter of Fiachna and chooses to remain in the Otherworld.

Conchobar and the Kingship of the Ulaid

This tale provides a short account of the method by which Conchobar mac Nessa inherited the kingship of the Ulaid. On the death of his father, Conchobar's mother Nessa daughter of Echaid was sought in marriage by Fergus king of the Ulaid. Nessa indicated that as a part of the bargain that she would not marry,

> "…not till I have a reward therefore, even a year's kingship for my son, so that my son may be called a king's son." [261]

Fergus agreed to this request and following the marriage, Nessa the Queen,

> "began instructing her son and the son's fosterers and his household to strip every second man, and to give (his wealth) to another, and her gold and her silver were given to the champions of the Ulaid, because of the result therof to her son." [262]

At the end of the year Fergus endeavoured to recover his Kingship but the Council sided with Conchobar. It was by this by this rouse the seven year old Conchobar became king of the Ulaid. Like many of the other pieces dealing with Kingship this story illustrates the pre-eminence and importance of shrewdness in the creation and maintenance of power.

On the First Poem made in Ireland

This is a very short verse in three quatrains attributed to Ai Mac Ollaman

It begins:

> "Question what was (the first) poem composed in Ireland, and who made it, and for whom was it made, and in what place was it made?
>
> There, then, the first poem was made, in Inis Tighe on Lough Corrib, in the west of Ireland; and he that made it was Ai son of Ollom, son of Delbaeth, and he made it for Fiacha son of Delbaeth the king of Ireland, his father's brother, and this is the poem"

Dealing with the early poets Dáibhí Ó Cróinín states

> "One of these tales the birth of Ai Mac Ollaman is a mythological 'charter' for the rights, privileges and status of poets." [263]

Ailim Bairc Mbraenaig

This piece consists of six lines of poetry which may have been included for literary and spatial reasons.

---

[261] Stokes, Whitley. Lives of Saints from the Book of Lismore. Oxford: Clarendon Press, 1890 pg. xxxiv.

[262] Do. pg. xxxiv.

[263] Ó Cróinín, Dáibhí [ed.] A new history of Ireland: Prehistoric and early Ireland Vol. I U.K.: Oxford University Press, 2005 1302p pg. 460.

Section XIII

The siege of Druim Dámgháire (Knocklong)

This is one of the longest pieces in the Codex and an accurate and readable version has been produced by Fermoy born Seán Ó Duinn. [264]   Its presence here has particular importance and as Ó Duinn comments *"the sole surviving manuscript containing the ancient Irish epic Forbuis Droma Dámgháire is found in the Book of Lismore"* [265]

The story relates the invasion of Munster by King Cormac Mac Art. It illustrates many of the preoccupations of early Irish epic literature of which the following are arbitrary examples. First we are presented with the power of the Druid as he evades his pursuers: *"When the druid became aware of this he turned to the stream and gave it three blows of the magic wand which he held in his hand so that it rose up in a deluge in front of the crowd. A large number had already gone over to the western side of the stream while another large group was actually in the river. The others pushed back and forth in an effort to rescue them. While all this was going on, the druid slipped away."* [266]

The importance of placenames [267] is explored as Cormac pitches his camp on a hillside: *"There is the clamour of the company and the loud yells of the crowd. Let the hill be known as Droim Dámgháire (the Ridge of the Assembly Calls) from today to eternity."* [268]   The organisation of military forces is described: *"The Munstermen selected 408 men in all. They were to be divided into groups of twenty with a single name for each group – that of the taoiseach (leader). The name which the taoiseach bore was also that of his group of twenty. The taoiseach was a fighter of twenty men and each man in his group was capable of fighting nine."* [269] And finally we have a local reference: *"The day came, however, when they were beside the River Siúir and Fiacha wanted to go for a swim. He took off his clothes and left his grey broadsided spear with Connla. Connla grasped the spear and struck Fiacha so that the spear penetrated through his body."* [270]

---

[264] *Forbhais Droma Dámgháire: The siege of Knocklong by Seán Ó Duinn Ireland: Mercier Press, 1992 111p.*

[265] *O'Duinn pg. 5.*

[266] *O'Duinn pg. 33.*

[267] *The centrality of placenames in early Irish literature is further attested by Thomas Kinsella in his introduction to "The Táin" where he states about this "phenomenon is not confined to the Táin, or the Ulster Cycle; it is a continuing preoccupation of early and medieval Irish literature, which contains a whole class of topographical works, including prose tracts and poems of enormous length..." Kinsella, Thomas. "The Táin: translated from the Irish Epic Táin Bó Cuailnge." Oxford University Press, 1970, xxvii, 283p pgs. xiii-xiv.*

[268] *Forbhais Droma Dámgháire: The siege of Knocklong by Seán Ó Duinn Ireland: Mercier Press, 1992 111p. pg. 41.*

[269] *O Duinn pg. 45.*

[270] *O Duinn pg. 111.*

Section XIV

Miscellaneous

Crichad an Chaoilli

"Crichad an Caoilli gu cruaidh
Ni bhfuil uaibh nech no imluaidh
Tucad do mac sonaisc sin
Ar an forbhais dfhoiridhin et cetera." [271]

This miscellaneous segment includes Crichad an Chaoilli or a tract on the Topography of Fermoy. Apart from its presence in the Book of Lismore this piece is only found in Egerton 92, fol. 13b. The text contains folios 140 and 141 and is one of the pieces stolen and later returned to the Book during the 19th Century. Canon Patrick Power has produced a comprehensive, exhaustive and erudite version [272] which includes a photographic reproduction of the text, a transliteration, a translation, profuse notes and a detailed introduction. His study has suffused, what on preliminary and superficial examination appears to be a dull and lifeless progress of names and places running to some 2000 words, with depths of meanings which cross the boundaries of time and place.

The tract is of ancient vintage and Power indicates it may predate the Synod of Rathbreasail which was held around 1110 A.D. He suggests the original compiler was dealing with period *"a century or two before his own time."* [273]

Caoille, an area of North East Cork, is alluded to little in the ancient texts and the placename may have evolved from the Irish word descriptive of a narrow plain between mountain ranges.

"Rare, however though use of the name Caoille be the region designated is well defined as the limestone plain which stretches south from the Ballyhoura and Galtee ranges to the parallel mountain chain of the Nagles and is bounded east and west by the Knockmealdowns and the Cork-Dublin railway line respectively." [274]

---

[271] *Crichad an Chaoilli: Being the topography of the ancient Fermoy. Edited with introduction translation, notes and map by Canon Patrick Power. Cork: Cork University Press, 1932. viii,135p. pg. 45.*

[272] *Do. pg. 45.*

[273] *Do. pg. 5.*

[274] *Do. pg. 6.*

It contains an area of roughly 250 sq miles. It was granted as is set out in *"The siege of Knocklong"* to the Druid Maigh Ruith. Its triuchas were reduced to 1 to contain the power of the owners. The triucha was originally a levy of 3000 men and *"had its prototype in the military organization of the Continental Celts."* [275] There were 10 Tuaths [276] within Caoille. In setting out the designated structure of Caoille Power indicates that the land extent within a triucha could vary and suggests that this tract is of particular interest as it *"shows us a triucha and various Tuaths in actual process of submergence."* [277]

Power's analysis of the tract is, as one would expect, fascinating in the interpretation of the placenames contained. There are 188 names indicating landowners, 109 physical landscapes, 58 artificial features (churches, etc.), 3 historical or legendary associations, and 6 others.

The piece contains extremely valuable indications of ecclesiastical history and has close links to the Lives of the Saints contained in the Book of Lismore. Power explores these references in detail and provides archaeological details on the remains proximate to the locations named. He suggests that the tract by virtue of the information provided on social conditions and church organization *"has quasi-imperative claims."* [278] Interestingly there are only 4 references to saints in the placenames of Caoille and of these Finnchu is particularly noteworthy as his life is contained in section on the lives of the saints. There are also references to the position of the Coarb. [279]

The exploration of the Carcar or Ogeen River which discharges itself into the Awbeg at Kilbarack near Doneraile is particularly interesting. While Power outlines the derivation from the Irish word for prison stating that it owes its name to fact of its *"disappearance underground during part of its course"* [280] he does not trace the origin of the word back to its Latin and undoubtedly ecclesiastical sources.

---

[275] *Do. pg. 17.*

[276] *The tuath was the next defined area below the Triucha.*

[277] *Do. pg. 17.*

[278] *Do. pg. vii.*

[279] *In medieval Ireland & Scotland the Co-arb or Coarb [alternatively "comarba"] was the president of a collegiate church [i.e. Celtic Monastery following the rule of St. Columba] who had the privilege of clerical orders and said mass 'serveth the cure']. As a successor of the founder of his order he had a seat in the mother church, a stall in the choir and a voice in the chapter. Although the Co-arb was in clerical orders, he was usually married, and if one of his sons was qualified by learning he would be chosen in time by the Dean and Chapter to be Co-arb. Thus the co-arbship was in a manner hereditary. After the reformation and the dissolution of the monasteries the role of co-arb became subsumed in that of the parish vicar.*

[280] *Do. pg. 101.*

In conclusion Power states:

> "A claim might fairly be made for our Topography of Fermoy that it is a document of unique character and scope. Indeed, we have no other document of the same precise class." [281]

Its distinctiveness lies in being *"an intensive study of a single petty princedom."* [282] It is worth noting that much of Power's information was sourced from local people and one wonders if we were to seek this information today how much would be retained in the folk memory of the local community.

Ba Faidh an Feinnidh bai Sunn
Truag Caiseal gan Chormac

These two poems concern the life and career of Cormac mac Cuilennáin king of Munster. The first is a poem ascribed to Cormac in eleven quatrains and *"composed by Cormac on a visit to Cenn Clair seat of Fiacha Muillethan…"* It is prefixed by a short pose preface:

> "Once upon a time, Cormac, son of Culennán, king of Munster, happened to go to Cenn Clairi; and this was why he went, that his mind might be commemorating every good thing that had been done there; and he composed the lay setting it forth." [283]

The poem describes some of the deeds of Mog Ruith the Druid and others. The second poem is a lament on the death of Cormac in thirteen quatrains.

Cormac was of the Eóganacht Chaisil and was a bishop prior to his accession as King of Munster in 902. Though renowned as a poet and scholar he was also a *"warrior king."* One of his campaigns in 907 waged in Leinster and Connacht is described in the Annals of Inisfallen. In 908, with his chief councillor Flaithbertach mac Inmainén, he embarked on a further campaign in Leinster and was killed at Bellach Mugna. His shrine is at Castledermot and was considered to have miraculous powers. He has been sometimes credited with the composition of Sanas Cormaic an early Irish glossary *"containing etymologies and explanations of over 1400 Irish words."* He is also credited with the Psalter of Cashel.

---

[281] *Do. pg. 34.*

[282] *Do. pg. 34.*

[283] *Lives of Saints from the Book of Lismore translated by Whitley Stokes Oxford: Clarendon Press, 1890 pg. xxxvi.*

Oilill Olom Amra an Ghein

This is a short poem of 10 quatrains listing the sons of Ailill Ólomm or Oilioll Olum. Ólomm was king of Munster during the 1st and 2nd Centuries A.D. He bore nineteen sons and this poem begins,

> *"Ailill Bare-ear, wondrous the birth,*
> *Son of Mugh Nudat the virulent:*
> *Nineteen sons, sprang from him*
> *Who divided themselves among the noble host."* [284]

The Annals recall his presence at the Battle of Ceannfeabhrat in 186 A.D. where his son Eoghain killed Dadera, Druid of the Dairinní. At the Battle of Magh Mucruimhe seven of his sons were killed, though Lady Gregory in *Gods and fighting men* [285] indicates that Oilioll himself was also killed there. Another son, Eochaidh Taebhfada, was killed at the Battle of Samhain in 241 A.D.

Oilioll Olum himself died in 234 A.D. according to the Annals. References and this account in the Book of Lismore can be directly attributed to the fact that it was from his son Eoghain that the Eóganacht ruling dynasty of Munster descended. This is the family from which the McCarthys directly sprang.

Bruiden Maic Dareo: The Story of Mac Dareo's Hostel

This is an intriguing and thematically enigmatic piece which is morally and ethically circumspect in its core methodology and message. Ostensibly a genealogy, it is really a device for dynastic succession validation and the extant versions inevitably convey opposing conclusions dependent on the dynastic support enjoyed by the writers. Eoin McNeill has provided a translation [286] of the most complete version that included in the Book of Fermoy. He specifically notes another version contained in the Book of Ballymote and references other versions but surprisingly does not mention that in the Book of Lismore which most probably had a common origin to the one in the Book of Fermoy.

---

[284] *Lives of Saints from the Book of Lismore translated by Whitley Stokes Oxford: Clarendon Press, 1890 pg. xxxvii.*

[285] *Gregory. Lady Augusta Gods and Fighting men 1904.*

[286] *Mac Neill, Eoin. Celtic Ireland. Dublin, Martin Lester Ltd., 1921 xv,182p pg.*

The key function of the narrative is to establish an aristocratic succession which is genealogically complete, chronologically consistent and demographically acceptable. To achieve this end there is a merging of mythical peoples regardless of temporal or practical inconsistencies and

> *"it is to be noted that, with a few noteworthy exceptions, the genealogies of the whole Gaelic race are traced to the three individual ancestors in the second century of the Christian era."* [287]

In setting out this thesis Mac Neill informs us that

> *"the descent of all the free Irish from Míl is a genealogical fiction of not earlier date than the seventh century…"* [288]

The key device used to achieve the desired conclusion is a massacre of the extant Irish aristocracy which consequently resolved the practical issues of genealogical and racial lines.

The story begins with an account of the unhappy state of the *"vassal peoples"* of Ireland, most prominently the Fir Bolg, in the period before the arrival of the Vikings:

> *"There was great murmuring among the vassal peoples of Ireland in the time of the three kings of Ireland, namely Fiacho Findolaidh, Fiac, son of Fidheccach, and Bres son of Ferbh. Fiacho Findolaidh, now, it was he who was king of Ireland at that time. Fiac son of Fidheccach was king of Munster. Bres, son of Ferbh, was king of the Ulidians."* [289]

Their central complaints concerned the levels of taxation and *"misrule"* by the Kings and ruling class. A gathering of the downtrodden was held at Mac Dareo's House in Bréifne and a decision was taken to massacre the entire aristocracy at a feast. The feast was arranged in Connaught but apparently held at Mac Dareo's House. Over 9000 were killed at the feast but three pregnant queens escaped, *"Side the Swift, and Crube (and Aine) they were."* [290] According to the narrator the three women who escaped were the daughters respectively of the kings of the *"three chief races of Britain: the Picts, the Britons and the Saxons…"* [291] This account ignores the fact that the Saxon occupation of England followed much later.

---

[287] *Do. pg. 2.*

[288] *Do. ["The revolt of the vassals" Chapter V pgs. 64-72] pg. 64.*

[289] *Do. ["The revolt of the vassals" Chapter V pgs. 64-72] pg. 65.*

[290] *Do. ["The revolt of the vassals" Chapter V pgs. 64-72] pg. 66.*

[291] *Do. ["The revolt of the vassals" Chapter V pgs. 64-72] pg. 69.*

The children of the Queens were reared in the east at a remove from King Cairbre the Ulidian who was elected by the vassal peoples. Famine, pestilence and bad weather followed for 20 years and on the death of Cairbre his son Morann refused the crown saying the three rightful heirs should return:

> "So they come from the East and each of them goes to his own place, to wit, Tipraite Tírech to the east of Ireland, to the fifth of the Ulaid, and Cairbre(=Corb) Ulom to its south, over Munster, Feradhach Find goes into the middle, to Temhair of the Kings. Then the sovereignty and the high-kingship of Ireland were given to Feradhach Find, and the headship in counsel and jurisprudence was given to Morann son of Maen [but son of Cairbre, above]." [292]

The rightful regal lines were thus re-established and the genealogical lines confirmed. According to Mac Neill,

> "it my be remarked that this early Gaelic nobility has no existence in the fabric of Milesian history except for the purpose of the massacre." [293]

And continuing he states that,

> "The 'Milesian' legend, like its name, is of Latin origin. It arises from an effort to find in Latin historical and geographical accounts of the world a suitable origin for the Gaelic people of Ireland." [294]

It is in this context that this short piece has a significant place in the historical annals of early Ireland.

---

[292] Do. ["The revolt of the vassals" Chapter V pgs. 64-72] pg. 67.

[293] Do. pg. 5.

[294] Do. pg. 6.

Poems

This sub-section includes a series of short poems whose key rationale for inclusion is probably literary and spatial. They are listed by Macalister as follows:

- *Abair dhamh ra Muimnechu* (author, Feidlimid mac Crimthainn)
- *Maithi Muman fa fir soin* (anonymous)
- *Eirigh frisin iarmeirghi* (Anonymous)
- *Cormac cofecht roba sai* (author, Lomaidhi)
- *In cloichen bec fuil im laimh* (author, Flaithbertach ua hInmoinén)
- *Tri ceimenn cindti do chách* (...ascribed to Adamnán)

The first is in 23 quatrains, the second in 13 quatrains and the third in 18 quatrains. The fourth in eight quatrains according to Stokes is entitled Lomaidhi. The fifth is in 13 quatrains and Stokes provides a translation of the first stanza of this:

> *The little pebble which is in my hand,*
> *O Overlord of the fair world!*
> *Many men have fallen by it,*
> *And another will fall."* [295]

The sixth poem is in only 3 quatrains and has been ascribed to Adamnán.

Stokes follows his description of this poem with a note in relation to a concluding sub-section for which no reference appears in Macalister's introduction and is consequently worth quoting in full:

> *"Story about a bishop Cainchomrac (ob. A.D. 901), who knew when everyone would die, and whether he would be rewarded or punished in the other world. Begins:*
>
> *'A noble bishop abode in Clonmacnois, Caincomrac was his name, and Mochta was his name at first. A son of virginity was he, and an heir of God, and on his pilgrimage he had gone to Clon(macnois.)'"* [296]

---

[295] *Lives of Saints from the Book of Lismore translated by Whitley Stokes Oxford: Clarendon Press, 1890 pg. xxxix.*

[296] *Lives of Saints from the Book of Lismore translated by Whitley Stokes Oxford: Clarendon Press, 1890 pg. xxxix.*

Psalter of the Pig: An Irish Legend [297]

There are five early versions of this tale and a sixth is contained in the book of Lismore. The central figure in Saltair na muice is Caenchomrac who was Abbot of the monastery of Louth. According to the Four Masters he died in 898.

Seeking solitude Caenchomrac moved to the vicinity of Lough Ree. This lake had been *"formed from the urine of a horse given to Ribh by the fairy King Mider."* [298] Under this lake is a monastery whose residents can visit the upper world and the monastery can in its turn be visited from the upper-world. This tale *"is more or less closely paralleled by many accounts of sunken churches, castles, and cities and of visits made by mortals to the subaqueous world in medieval romance and in modern folk-lore."* [299]

"Early Celtic tradition is particularly rich in accounts of uncanny swine. One of oldest and best-known stories is that of the pigs of Derbrenn, which were human beings transformed into animals." [300] In this story Caenchomrac is presented with gifts by the people of Teffia and area of modern Longford Westmeath. He in turn offers in return the following prediction:

> *"Nine men out of melodious Teffia*
> *Against (?) a hundred thousand of thousands –*
> *Let them think on Caenchomrac*
> *Verily they shall reach safety."* [301]

In the gifts he receives Caenchomrac sets to cook pigs that have been killed on Slieve Leitrim. However, these are in fact men transformed into pigs and the father of one returns to regain the body. He brings the son's Psalter *"for if he himself now lived, it is well he would have arranged the psalm-singing"* [302] [– hence the title Psalter of the pig.] Caenchomrac visits the monastery under sea with the father and remained there *"from one canonical hour till the corresponding one next day performing canonical service and mass."* [303] On his return he chides his monks for eating bacon in Lent *"and from that time forth the wise ones of the Gael have never eaten flesh on Maundy Thursday."* [304]

---

[297] *Cross, Tom Peete. Modern Philology Vol. 18 no. 8 December 1920 pp.443-455.*

[298] *Do. pg. 446.*

[299] *Do. pg. 446-447.*

[300] *Do. pg. 447.*

[301] *Do. pg. 450.*

[302] *Do. pg. 451.*

[303] *Do. pg. 451.*

[304] *Do. pg. 452.*

Section XV

The progress of the burdensome troop

A section of miscellaneous material including Imtheacht na trom dáimhé or the Adventures of the Great Company which tells the story of the Great Filé Senchán's attempt to retrieve the tale of the Táin Bó Chuailgné.

Tromdám Guaire: (The Progress of the Burdensome Troop) [305]

More than any other tract in the Book of Lismore, Tromdám Guaire, appears an amalgam of sources and styles compiled over a lengthy period but possessing extraordinary depth, sophistication and containing little not carefully considered, crafted and distilled. In his seminal study Seán Ó Coileáin suggests that the work is:

> *"More than anything else it is a literary tale, the product of the amused and sceptical outlook of a reasonably well-read man"* [306]

He then suggests that the work is of the *"late thirteenth or early fourteenth century."* [307] James Carney in his *"polemic"* study [308] divides the work into three sections: Introduction; The Contention; The Quest. While most versions contain two recensions, *"there is a third recension in which the story of the poet's visitation is told at length. It is preserved in the Book of Lismore."* [309] This recension presents the complete text.

In outline the tract commences with a dispute between Aed son of Dua the Black king of Oriel and Fergna king of Bréifne. King Fergna entices the poet Dallán to seek Aed's shield Duibgilla for a poetic recitation and suggests that if the King is unwilling to part with the shield he should be threatened with satire. Aed refuses and is cursed and satirised. Dallán on leaving Oriel recovers his sight, dies and is replaced by Senchán. However, in his study Ó Coileáin tells us that Dallán *"had originally recovered his sight for the purpose of composing a eulogy whereas in the Tromdám it is due to the composition of an unjust but equally obscure satire."* [310]

---

[305] *Tromdám Guaire: The great visitation to Guaire from "The Cycles of the Kings" by Myles Dillon Oxford University Press, 1946 pgs. 90-98.*

[306] *The making of Tromdám Guaire. Seán Ó Coileáin. Ériu: Founded as the Journal of the School of Irish Learning devoted to Irish Philology and Literature. Vol. XXVIII. Dublin: Royal Irish Academy, 1977 pgs. 32-70. pg. 35.*

[307] *Do. pg. 69.*

[308] *Carney, James. Studies in Irish literature and History. Dublin: Institute for Advances Studies, 1966.*

[309] *Tromdám Guaire: The great visitation to Guaire from "The Cycles of the Kings" by Myles Dillon Oxford University Press, 1946 pgs. 90-98 pg. 90.*

[310] *The making of Tromdám Guaire. By Seán Ó Coileáin in Ériu: Founded as the Journal of the School of Irish Learning devoted to Irish Philology and Literature. Vol. XXVIII. Dublin Royal Irish Academy, 1977 pgs. 32-70. pg. 40.*

Senchán following his elevation sets out to visit king Guaire with his full entourage and *"the poets demanded various things difficult to obtain so as to dishonour him. But he was enabled by the favour of God and the assistance of the saintly swineherd Marbán."* [311] One such demand is made on behalf of Muirenn widow of Dallán who:

> *"required a bowl of new milk with the marrow of a wild pig's trotter; a pet cuckoo singing on a tree beside her, although it was then between Christmas and Little Christmas; a full load of the lard of a white boar tied on her back; a roan horse to ride on, and a cloak made of spider's webs; and that she might so ride into Durlas humming a tune."* [312]

Her demand is satisfied through the intersession of Marbán whose pet boar is killed as part of the demand. However, Muirenn subsequently dies in consequence, and Marbán vows vengeance on all the poets. Marbán comes to Durlas and seeks from the poets *"humming,"* but specifically that *"called crónán snagach"* which is very exhausting. Following the unsuccessful efforts of some of the minor poets Senchán has to meet the demand and in his effort to hum, *"one of Senchán's eyes leaped from its socket on to his cheek."* This eye is replaced by Marbán but he then seeks a recitation of the Táin. None of the poets can meet this demand and:

> *"I put you under gesa until you tell me the Táin and I put all the Great Visitation under gesa if they stay two nights in the same house until they discover the Táin"* [313]

Prior to his departure on the quest Senchán recites a lay in which he outlines the sheer scale of the Great Visitation and concludes:

> *"I declare to thee, O God*
> *Who canst the promise verify,*
> *That should we return to our own land*
> *We shall visit thee again, O Guaire, though now we depart."*

The search includes Britain and is unsuccessful Senchán finally seeks the intersession of Caillín. He and the other Saints of Ireland visit Durlas raise Fergus and he recites the Táin which is then written down by Ciarán of Clonmacnoise. In an alternative version [314] the Táin is recovered by Muiren son of Senchán and a bard named Eimena who come across a standing stone near a lake in Connaught. Then as related by Samuel Ferguson:

> *"And with joy and wonder thrilling, part a-thrill with fear,*
> *Muirgen read the legend plainly, 'Fergus son of Roy is here.'"*

---

[311] *Tromdám Guaire: The great visitation to Guaire from "The Cycles of the Kings" by Myles Dillon Oxford University Press, 1946 pgs. 90-98 pg. 90.*

[312] *Do. pg. 92-93.*

[313] *Do. pg. 95.*

[314] *Shallcrass, Philip: A little history of Ogham.*

This Ogham version is also recounted by Rolleston who states that *"it was believed to have been written out in Ogham characters on staves of wood, which a bard who possessed them had taken with him to Italy, whence they never returned."* [315] Rolleston then comments on the recovery: *"At last Sanchan sent his son Murgen with his younger brother Eimena to journey to Italy and endeavour to discover there the fate of the staff-book."* [316] He concludes with a quote from Ferguson:

> *"So it comes, the lay, recover'd once at such a deadly cost,*
> *Ere one full recital suffer'd, once again is all but lost:*
> *For the maiden's malediction still may a blemish-stain*
> *Clings in coarser garb of fiction round the fragments that remain."* [317]

Following the recovery and the recitation to Marbán the poets are entertained and then Marbán issues his judgement:

> *"The judgement that I pronounce on you .is that each ollam shall return to his own territory and that there shall be no Great Visitation in future'…and the Great Visitation travelled no more in Ireland ever since."* [318]

Ó Coileáin in his study [319] suggests that the primary object of the author was *"is in creation not in preservation."* He makes several interesting points and while quoting Carney's assertion that

> *"Marbán is ultimately none other than the Gaelic-British St. Kentigern, who for saga purposes has become a naturalised Irishman"* [320]

he discounts this and proceeds to significant lengths to offer alternatives including marbh[an] or a diminutive of dead; a dead giant-corpse. He praises the work despite its many plagiarisms but states that it *"is finally its own original."* In conclusion he states:

> *"The work is completely untypical of medieval Irish literature in general in the attitudes it adopts towards earlier tradition."* [321]

---

[315] *Rolleston, T.W. Myths and legends of the Celtic Race. London: George Harrap & Company, 1912. pgs. 234-238. pg. 234.*

[316] *Do. pg. 234.*

[317] *Do. pg, 238.*

[318] *Tromdám Guaire: The great visitation to Guaire from "The Cycles of the Kings" by Myles Dillon Oxford University Press, 1946 pgs. 90-98 pg. 98.*

[319] *The making of Tromdám Guaire. By Seán Ó Coileáin in Ériu: Founded as the Journal of the School of Irish Learning devoted to Irish Philology and Literature. Vol. XXVIII. Dublin Royal Irish Academy, 1977 pgs. 32-70.*

[320] *Do. pg. 46.*

[321] *Do. pg. 69.*

Airem Muintiri Finn: The Enumeration of Finn's People [322]

This piece contains a list of the athletic and other feats required for entry to the Fianna led by Fionn Mac Cumhaill. It also contains a list of his followers. The Fianna was a body of *"seven score and ten officers, each man of these – having thrice nine warriors* and a key rule was that *"no single individual of them to fly before nine warriors."*

For those seeking entrance *"not a man was taken until he were a prime poet versed in the twelve books of poesy."* They must be able to repel *"nine warriors, having nine spears"* and must also be able to run through Ireland's woods pursued, avoid wounds during the pursuit and also not crack *"a dry stick under his foot."*

The Fianna served *"the seventh king ruling Ireland: that is to say there were five kings of the provinces, and the king of Ireland; he being himself the seventh conjointly with the king of all Ireland."*

Amongst those listed as the followers of Fionn are *"Cudam; his two spear-bearers: and Uadgarb; his shield-bearer."*

Bliadhuin don Chuailli, III Bliadna don Gurt

This is a short and intriguing poem, without a title, which outlines the relative life spans of some flora, fauna and man. The extract below will suffice to illustrate:

> *"Three lifetimes of the horse for the human being.*
> *Three lifetimes of the human being for the stag.*
> *Three lifetimes of the stag for the ousel.*
> *Three lifetimes of the ousel for the eagle."* [323]

From the information provided it *"can be inferred that the Irish of the eleventh century held four of the oldest animals to be the stag, the wild boar, the hawk and the salmon."* [324] It is difficult to see significant rationale for its inclusion in the text.

Ben Ro la Muir Inn Albain

This is a very short piece which has been damaged and only some of the text is legible.

> *"There came a woman upon the shore of Scotland this year. Twelve feet and nine score was her length: sixteen the length of her tress: seven feet the length of her fingers: six the length of her nose. Whiter than a swan or the foam of a wave was her body."* [325]

Accounts of the event are also given in the Chronicon Scotorum [A.D. 900}, The Annals of Ulster [A.D.890], the Annals of the Four Masters [A.D.887] and the Annals of Inisfallen [A.D.892]. Whether its value and interest is linguistic or allegorical is not apparent.

---

[322] *Airem muintiri Finn: The enumeration of Finn's People. Translated by Standish O'Grady. Silva Gadelica Vol. II.*

[323] *Stokes, Whitley. Lives of the Saints from the Book of Lismore pg. xli.*

[324] *Do. pg. xli.*

[325] *Stokes, Whitley. Lives of Saints from the Book of Lismore. Oxford: Clarendon Press, 1890. pg. xlii.*

An Agallamh Bheag

An Agallamh Bheag is a rare piece and the only manuscripts which are known to contain it are the Book of Lismore and the Reeves MS. [326] Douglas Hyde has suggested that it is the *"beginning hitherto lost, of the long story of the 'Colloquy with the Ancients."* [327] However, the atmosphere of depression and fatalistic acquiescence which pervades it is not so prevalent or obvious in the Ancients and it might perhaps be described as a prequel with a distinct and separate theme and flavour. It is undoubtedly a most powerful evocation of the passing of the pre-Christian era and its sadness is profound.

The events described precede those portrayed in the Ancients and take place in the period after the arrival of St. Patrick. They concern the transformation of Ireland when *"all that were left of the Fenians: namely Ossian and Cailte and [twenty-seven of their followers] three groups of nine each…"* [328]

The Fianna have been displaced and most of their number is dead. They have fled to remote areas and live in great fear and uncertainty. While on a hunting expedition one of their gilley's encounters a great host and *"this was their description: fair, bright cloaks of linen were around them; their heads were pierced; they had bent staves in their hands; and thick, variegated shields of bright gold and of silver were upon their breasts"* [329] as they proceed they chant *"each single man of them."* He is greatly influenced and impacted by this chance encounter and is filled *"with the pain of heavy sickness at the breathing of that troop."* The arrival of these *"Adze-heads"* [330] had been foretold by Finn. This short but powerful section vividly describes the supplementation of the era of the druids and the civilization they represented by the early Christian period. The Fianna recognize that unless this host is eradicated *"they will rule over us."* However, Ossian in a startling lament acknowledges that their time has already passed: *"Alas!…it is not ourselves who are in possession of the kingship of Ireland, with its drinking and with its joy; but rather [we have] only its hunting and its wild places and its forests; and it will be better for us to avoid them."* [331]

---

[326] *Pennington, Walter. "The Little colloquy. Philological Quarterly Volume IX, April 1930 Number 2. pgs. 97-111, pg. 97.*

[327] *Do. pg. 97.*

[328] *Do. pg. 97.*

[329] *Do. pg. 98.*

[330] *The Adz is a cutting tool of the general shape of a grubbing hoe, having an edge across the end of a blade set in a plane at right angles to the handle.*

[331] *Pennington, Walter. "The Little colloquy. Philological Quarterly Volume IX, April 1930 Number 2. pgs. 97-111, pg. 99.*

His lament contains a beautiful and evocative simile in which he is not dismissive of the positive benefits of Christianity, *"Ireland is as quiet as a frozen pool"* and *"there is no outlaw or man slayer or forest robber in Ireland."* The sub text might suggest that the Fianna have been rendered redundant.

As they observe the smoke from the camp fires of the *"Adze-heads"* they realize their time has passed and Cailte recites a profound lay which outlines their dilemma:

> *"Our three nine of men of the grey-haired Fenians;*
> *That there would arise a matter there to disperse us;*
>
> *To us its evil would be lasting*
> *Ossian, son of Finn, shall go from us,*
> *And nine men under the water of Adze-head"* [332]

He sees that they will accept baptism and the Fenians *"shall be scattered throughout the desolate mountains"* by –

> *"The Adze-head who has come from the East*
> *To drive out the druids of the world;"*

While they consider vengeance, Ossian takes a step forward to attack the camp but only his own eight men follow him and *"nine men including Cailte went into the woods and tickets and into the wild places of Ireland; and nine others fled to the fairy mounds of Ireland before the Adze-head."* [333]

The rationale for this split is provided by Cailte who suggests that Ossian will *"be coaxed or deceived, and he will believe under the yoke of baptism and faith. Anyone who does not desire to believe in them, let him no approach them."* [334] The split is irrevocable and only Cailte and Ossian will meet again. This encounter is described in the Ancients when they meet at the palace of Tara with King Cerbhuill.

That the rendition is provided by old men is testified by their view of the hunting prowess of the present generation, *"each generation of men is worse than the one before it."* [335] One last attempt to interface with the modern world is provided when they meet Irgal mac Muradhaigh King of Chorc Dhuibhne who is happy with the world he inhabits as *"Ireland is full of every kind of prosperity."* Irgal seeks a *"hunting-charm"* which precipitates the removal of his rival, Ceallach mac Sealba subsequent to single combat in which Irgal defeats and slays him.

---

[332] *Do. pg. 101.*

[333] *Do. pg. 101.*

[334] *Do. pg. 101.*

[335] *Do. pg. 105.*

Irgal's wife Dubh-Gréine eves-drops on a discussion between Irgal and the Fenians in which Irgal seeks a charm to enable the expulsion of black-birds which are damaging Irgal's corn. This will mean that *"for all living things which are proclaimed in this charm, from the rising till the setting of the sun, will be dead within nine days unless they depart this place within a day."* [336]

But Dearg Gréine first recites the incantation *"upon yourselves be the poison and danger of your charm."* She then flees but is killed in a fall and the Fenians are forced to leave and *"let not anyone come to us after Irgal"* and they flee to a deserted glen. The message conveyed in this final encounter would suggest that magic of the druids has no place in a selfish and uncaring world.

One final and important piece of dinnseanchas provided and concludes the piece as on arrival at the Glen one of the Fianna asks *"Why is this fort before us called 'The little fort of Wonder?'"* [337] In a diluted response we are informed that a *"dog brighter than snow"* bathes in a pool within the glen and *"one of the curious things about that dog is that the water into which he was put became wine or mead."*

Agallamh na Senórach

Agallamh na Senórach tells the epic story of Finn Mac Cumhaill and the Fianna. It *"is normally dated by scholars to the end of the twelfth century, though the present translators consider the early thirteenth century as a more likely date."* [338] There are four primary sources for the tales but most cogently the translators of the version from which this text was prepared state that the *"most complete is that contained in the Book of Lismore."* [339] The Book of Lismore also contains *"The little colloquy"* which is of later vintage possibly dating from the 14th or early 15 century. *"It is this later Acallamh which was copied repeatedly in the paper manuscripts of the modern period."* [340]

According to Ann Dooley the Colloquy with the ancient men *"is the longest original literary text in medieval Irish literature…"* [341] It explores two central strands of Celtic Folklore, firstly the *"extremely important genre of Dinnseanchas"* [topography] and secondly Patrician hagiography.

---

[336] *Do. pg. 109.*

[337] *Do. pg. 111.*

[338] *Tales of the elders of Ireland (Acallamh na Senórach) translated with an introduction and notes by Ann Dooley & Harry Roe. Oxford University Press, 1999 xxxlviii, 245p pg. viii.*

[339] *Tales pg. xxxi.*

[340] *Tales. pg. xxxi.*

[341] *Tales pg. viii.*

It is in many ways didactic and *"indeed Tales itself may be seen as an instructional tool of some subtlety in the effort to reform the social fabric"* [342] of the Ireland of the day. It should be notes that while the events portrayed are centuries before the writer's time the text *"For all its romanticism and heroic nostalgia the text presents itself as an instrument of vital engagement with a very real world."* [343]

In style the Tales were revolutionary: *"As a literary invention, nothing quite like Tales had appeared before in Irish literary tradition."* [344] There is a mixing of characters and times and the text moves from one period to another without concern for synchronicity of chronology and *"it is this cavalier treatment of the 'canonical' materials of learned tradition that releases the text and allows it to convey meanings of a more up-to-date kind"* [345] It is interesting that the events are structured around a journey and parallels with the *Odyssey* can be drawn in what is also a voyage of self discovery.

The tales of the Fianna later received major attention during the European Romantic Period and were *"fully implicated in the evolution of eighteenth-century aesthetic values, in the concept of original genius, of theories of the passions, and the cult of natural feeling these heroic figures from a Celtic past penetrated deeply into the heart of European and American romantic and revolutionary movements."* [346] The tales can *"be regarded as a fully fledged work of European chivalric romance where values of refined love between hero and heiress are worked out, albeit tragically, in a uniquely Irish literary fashion."* [347]

The text deals with the Fianna who were a landless warrior caste awaiting inheritance to family possessions or roles in the event of the deaths of their older siblings. The text also refers to previous conquerors of Ireland including the Fír bolg and Túatha Dé Dannan. The elders of the title are the last remnants of the Fianna and central to the tale are Caílte and Oisín the son of Finn. The important place of music and storytelling is explored and as the tales are narrated to Saint Patrick who makes *"many endorsements of the benefits and the aesthetic value of the Fenian tales"* [348] we can assume a deliberate blending of traditions.

---

[342] *Tales pg. xxix.*

[343] *Tales pg. xxx.*

[344] *Tales pg. xx.*

[345] *Tales pg. xxi.*

[346] *Tales pg. vii.*

[347] *Tales pg. xxvi.*

[348] *Tales pg. xvii.*

The place of the musician was extremely important in early Irish society and *"the greatest significance of Cas Corach's* [349] *achievement, however, is the witness it bears to the coming together of music and story-telling in a new genre of performance."* [350] This covers the development of the *"lay"* into Celtic and sub sequentially into continental use as *"shot verse-narrative pieces accompanied by music."* [351]

Druids and magic are essential themes and the magical qualities of watercress are pursued. Within the first tales there are references to Artúir the Briton. Reference made to the Land of the Maidens can surely be paralleled to a similar abode mentioned in Marco Polo. There is one local reference to hunting on Sliabh Gua. [352] Throughout the tales the importance of numerics is expressed and in typical poetic phrasing on one occasion Finn says *"If nine* [353] *warriors cast nine tall, riveted spears at him he catches them all without a scratch or scrape on him, and if, at the same time, nine balls are cast at him he catches them all in one hand with one of them touching the ground"* [354]

Finally, the centrality of placenames in Irish tradition is displayed *"Why is this place called the Oakwood of the Conspiracy and why is the ridge called the Ridge of the Dead Woman, and why is this little fort in front of us to the south called the Little Fort of the Incantation?"* [355]

---

[349] *The chief musician of the Tales.*

[350] *Tales pg. xix.*

[351] *Tales pg. xix.*

[352] *Tales pg. 155.*

[353] *The number nine had a huge symbolic significance in Celtic Mythology.*

[354] *Tales pg. 163.*

[355] *Tales pg. 166.*

Conclusion

In pursuing the Book of Lismore as a source of serious research and study one's first instinct was that it would represent an exciting source for the examination of early and medieval Irish Civilization and in this respect it does not disappoint with key areas of folklore, topography, placenames, [356] genealogies and hagiography well represented. However, as with all projects, when one peeks below the surface, there are central precepts that determine the nature, scale and importance of the Book of Lismore. Seminal to these are the twin themes of Education and Canonicity.

It is important to place The Book of Lismore in the context of early Irish and Celtic education. Formal education in Celtic societies has been traced to the 2nd Century B.C. and *"Celtic society was organised along hierarchical lines, being divided into four main classes: those of scholars, warriors, farmers and common workers. It was from the first of these classes, that of the Druids or scholars, that education was provided."* [357]

It is essential to state that the Druids were primarily teachers and even Julius Caesar commenting on this role states *"Because they did not want their doctrine to become public property, and in order to prevent their pupils from relying on the written word and neglecting to train their memories; for it is usually found that when people have the help of texts they are less diligent in learning by heart and let their memories rust."* [358] As Chadwick has commented *"The outstanding feature of the druidical teaching may be summed up as natural philosophy and natural science – the nature of the physical universe and its relationship to mankind."* [359] This system evolved into the Bardic schools which continued up to the 17th Century. In tandem with the secular tradition the Missionary School System developed. It has been suggested that Ireland had no written tradition until the event of Christianity with the notable exception of the Ogham System, from Ogma the druidic goddess of eloquence. The Monastic schools appeared by the 6th century and these represents a certain fusion with Bardic traditions. In fact *"two leading scholars in the field, Ryan and Gougaud, have both attributed the special character of Celtic monasticism to its assimilation of the native cultural traditions that preceded it."* [360]

---

[356] Celts and specifically Druids saw the gods in places and led to their practice of worshipping rivers mountains etc. – *"This eventually found expression in the romantic celebration of place which is so significant a feature of the poetic legacy they passed on to the Bardic writers"* Murphy, pg. 10.

[357] A history of Irish emigrant and missionary education. Daniel Murphy. Ireland: Four Courts Press, 2000. pg. 2.

[358] Murphy, pgs 3-4.

[359] The Druids. Nora Chadwick & Anne Ross. U.K.: University of Wales Press; (Rev. Edition), 1997. 119p.

[360] Murphy, pg. 22.

These schools and the monasteries to which they were attached were not reclusive establishments and large numbers of lay and foreign students studied within them. In fact, Hughes has pointed out *"In eight century Ireland the proportion of literate laymen must have been abnormally high when compared with the rest of Europe."* [361]   It was here that the monks engaged in a range of aesthetic activities such as manuscript illumination, calligraphy, and musical composition.

In these schools the number of those studying from Europe as well as transmissions from the Irish abroad led to huge cross-fertilisation of European literature. The availability of literature was essential and as Europe emerged from the dark ages this was a major problem as is evidenced by the first *"lengthy and detailed medieval library catalogue was compiled at Reichenau in the year 821 or 822.*

> *It survives today only in a printed edition based on an old copy, now lost. According to this catalogue, which is arranged by author or subject matter, Reichenau's library contained at that time over 400 volumes."* [362]

At the heart of the Irish monastic tradition and curriculum was grammar which *"According to the educational programme and ideals inherited from late antique Christianity, grammar was the first of the seven artes liberales and was the first step on the path which led to divina sapientia."* [363]   In the search for material to study the attitude of monasteries towards the classics was essentially that despite the profane nature of some of the subject matter the art of the composition overruled religious reservations. In this regard the Book of Lismore can be seen as a key element in, and product of the educational thinking of the time. Without doubt, virtually every piece conforms to this purpose of education and enlightenment and as an illustration one could suggest that the presence of Marco Polo at the dawn of the Age of Discovery is by no means accidental.

Finally the Book of Lismore raises interesting questions on the evolution of Literary Canons. *"The Greek-originated term canon, first applied in the context of the assimilation of religious literature into the Jewish Torah and Christian Bible, has been used increasingly in our generation to refer to bodies of authoritative or paradigmatic secular literature."* [364]   While woodblock printing in China had *"brought a corpus a significantly higher measure of stability and durability"* and allowed also for more widely reproduction and dissemination of specific texts, until the event of printing in Europe the manuscript tradition continued to allow for much variation in texts.

---

[361] *The Church in early Irish society. U.K.: Methuen, 1966. xii, 303p. [quoted in Murphy pg. 27.].*

[362] *Manuscripts and libraries in the Age of Charlemagne. Bernard Bischoff. U.K.: Cambridge University Press, 2007. pgs 96-97.*

[363] *Manuscripts and libraries in the Age of Charlemagne. Bernard Bischoff. U.K.: Cambridge University Press, 2007. pg. 105.*

[364] *Buddhist Canonicities: Value and evaluation in the digital age. By Charles Muller, Toyo Gakuen University. [online article] pg. 1.*

This is apparent in the Book of Lismore where it appears that *"good stories"* were integrated into unrelated text and a key concern was an underlying principle of making the maximum use of what was a very valuable commodity, namely vellum.

There is a critical additional factor in Medieval Ireland civilization as we must not only consider the major variations in our classic manuscripts but also the overriding centrality of the oral tradition. In a remarkable paper [365] Joseph Falaky Nagy condenses and re-evaluates many of the competing approaches to the evolution of, and relationships between, oral and literary traditions in early Ireland.

For the first school of thought, in which James Carney has played a central role, primacy and superiority is granted to the written medium but the variations and shortcomings apparent in the manuscript sources are unequivocally attributed to the oral tradition. Carney accepts that there was significant alteration in the transfer to the written form and suggests that this alteration in presentation was *"worthy of the new degree of sophistication which their society had attained by the very fact of becoming literate."* [366] While accepting the disparate and alternative need of each medium, he quite correctly disputes the *"notion of oral tradition as a static repository for authorised texts."* He suggests that evolution of texts occurred through a process of *"conflation,"* or a coming together of disparate but related and sympathetic constituent originals. As Nagy summarises:

> *"The medieval transmitter of literature may not always have treated the text as fixed, partly because he wanted to incorporate multiform oral material, and partly because he viewed or mentally 'heard' certain types of passages in the written text in terms of oral performance."* [367]

Carney's thesis finds ultimate expression in the work of Alan Bruford who proposes that *"the Romantic tales are so complex that they are hardly likely to have been preserved in any other way than writing."* [368] In this he totally rejects the parallel and synergetic development of the media over a prolonged period of time. However, what is undoubtedly true is that canonicity is more validly a feature of the written and specifically the printed *"text."*

The second school, on the other hand, holds that the social status and tradition of oral presentation and performance together with an undoubted ability to incorporate Indo-European influences and a facility for improvisation was ideally suited to the Irish psyche.

[365] Nagy, Joseph Falaky. *Orality in Medieval Irish Narrative: An overview. Oral Tradition 1-2 1986 pgs. 272-301.*

[366] Carney, James. *Studies in Irish Literature and History. Dublin: Institute for Advanced Studies, 1955. pg. 276-277.*

[367] Nagy, Joseph Falaky. *Orality in Medieval Irish Narrative: An overview. Oral Tradition 1-2 1986 pg. 289.*

[368] Bruford, Alan. *Gaelic folktales and medieval romances: A study of early Modern Irish 'Romantic tales and their oral derivatives. Dublin: Institute for Advanced Studies, 1966.*

In a further development on this theme, Cecile O'Rahilly, commenting on the Táin one of the longest of the sagas, sees its episodic and "uneven and lopsided" nature as an illustration that *"suggested that the native genius of the Irish writer is better suited to the short story than a work of long and complicated structure."* [369] This thesis finds a modern echo in *"Luck and the Irish"* by Roy Foster who has indicated just such a basis in the modern Irish penchant for the short story rather than the novel.

Central to the argument is the status of the poets, *"paradigms of social behaviour and an ideological world-view."* In Ireland, unlike the experience in other cultures where oral transmission existed at a lower status level than the written:

> *"the Irish oral tradition embraced the literature of greatest social prestige, as well as the common lore of the mass of the people."* [370]

It not only existed on at least an equal footing with but also incorporated valuable substance from the literary medium. In developing this theme Mac Cana turns the argument on its head suggesting that the earlier literati were making *"attempts to forge a literary style out of elements of the prevailing oral style."* This precept is developed in Gerard Murphy's crucial study which contrasts the sophistication, longevity and social status of the oral tradition and the first attempts at literary transmission in Ireland:

> *"we can be fairly certain that the tales, as really told to assembled kings and noblemen at an ancient óenach [assembly], were very different from the poorly-narrated manuscript versions noted down by monastic scribes as a contribution to learning rather than to literature."* [371]

A central feature of the oral tradition as set out by Myles Dillon is that *"the verse passages of direct speech were fixed as canonical and memorised, and the narrative was left to the creative memory of the reciter."* [372] This not only left scope for but in fact virtually prescribed improvisation thus ensuring that *"variations and cruces"* were

> *"not the result of scribed invention, error, or inflation of previously existing versions, but instead a reflection of the multiformity in the tradition of oral performance existing behind and alongside the texts and the literary tradition which created and transmitted them."* [373]

---

[369] O'Rahilly, Cecile. *Táin Bó Cúalnge* Dublin: Institute for Advanced Studies, 1967. *pg. xxv.*

[370] Mac Cana, Proinsias. *Irish Literary Tradition. In A view of the Irish Language.* Ed. By Brian Ó Cuív Dublin: Stationery Office, 1969.

[371] Murphy, Gerard. *Saga and myth in Ancient Ireland. Orig. published 1955. reprinted in Early Irish Literature* Eleanor Hull and Gerard Murphy London: Routledge & Keegan Paul, 1966. *pg. 99.*

[372] Dillon, Myles *Celts and Aryans: Survivals of Indo-European Speech and Society.* Simla: Indian Institute of Advanced Study, 1975. *pgs. 78-79.*

[373] Nagy, Joseph Falaky. *Orality in Medieval Irish Narrative: An overview. Oral Tradition 1-2 1986 pg. 278.*

A further facet is the centrality and omnipotence of *"memory"* as expressed in the Táin where *"we find the implicit message that the availability of written texts can corrupt filidecht and the storyteller's membair."* [374] Without doubt, the contents of the Book of Lismore studied as a unit and related to other major Irish and Celtic manuscripts provides an extraordinarily valuable resource for the interpretation of the movement from an oral to a written transmission of folklore, heritage and civilization in early and medieval Ireland.

---

[374] *Nagy, Joseph Falaky. Orality in Medieval Irish Narrative: An overview. Oral Tradition 1-2 1986 pg. 292.*

Index